A Note to the Reader

This book was written in the early 1950's by Earl D. Hunter, a missionary assigned to Guatemala in 1946 by the Church of the Nazarene. The title of the book is important because it refers to Rev. Hunter's service as an Army Chaplain during World War II. Imagine the adjustment of transitioning from war time to service in the jungles of Central America. This was the era of the DC3 aircraft, the new wonder drug penicillin, a jeep as the only vehicle, and a Johnson outboard motor to use with a dugout canoe.

Today it is possible to visit the same place in Guatemala and find both people and living conditions transformed in ways that could not be imagined in the early 1950's.

It is important to keep in mind that perspectives of many things were different in the 1940's and 1950's. So enjoy this first person account by someone that was "there."

Earl D. Hunter died a few months before his 100th birthday in 2015.

Contents

CHAPTER I	The Primitive Lacondones............5
CHAPTER II	Meet Some Native Christians........9
CHAPTER III	Exploring the Jungle....................15
CHAPTER IV	Going Native......................................23
CHAPTER V	Forming a Church..........................28
CHAPTER VI	Healing the Sick 32
CHAPTER VII	Comforting the Bereaved.........41
CHAPTER VIII	Introducing Native Pastors.....45
CHAPTER X	Four Great Needs...........................55
CHAPTER X	Four Effective Cures 77
CHAPTER XI	The Heavenly Vision 97
CHAPTER XII	The Harvest...............................114

CHAPLAIN IN THE JUNGLE

Missionary Stories
From the Guatemalan Jungles

By

Earl D. Hunter

Copyright 2019 – Sam Hunter
son of Earl D. Hunter
All rights reserved

Dedicated to the lady
who has shared it all
with piety, love, and humor.

CHAPTER I
The Primitive Lacondones

As we stood amidst the ruins of the prehistoric Mayan culture and then penetrated the jungles to visit the last remnant of that fallen race in Lacondon, I solemnly wondered what act of God eliminated them. Dwelling not too far from these primitive people and often sharing for days at a time a similar way of life, I was reminded of a childhood dream that someday I might be in a world where I would be the only one who had experienced the advantages of our modern world full of books and gadgets. Perhaps that is why I have always been obsessed with an urge to learn the fundamentals of everything. Here among the Lacondones, of Guatemala, I was to have this experience.

We found the primitive Lacondones, after a short hike from the new airstrip, living in the finest, densest jungle I know of. Their trails are not much more perceptible than the roads of the leafcutting ants. Contrary to the best available sources of information, we found that there was only one family of these people living on the Guatemala side of the Usumacinte River. There are perhaps two hundred in all, but they are so nearly nomadic that they cross over into Mexico without the slightest concern for the international boundary stipulations. They seem to be peaceful people.

While they are doubtless direct descendants from the long since extinct Mayan civilization, they have lost almost all trace of the high culture that once built the great cities with thirtystory temples and left wonderfully sculptured steles and made writings in hieroglyphics which remain to be read.

Our Christian interpreter, who spoke Maya, greeted the family and walked into their house without formalities. He immediately told them of our mission. It wasn't long until we saw him showing them with outstretched hands how Christ had been crucified. The men had previously attended several preaching services but we were unable to know just how much help they had received from the services.

They seemed to feel honored by our visit and the oldest man acted as spokesman, as he was clearly the highest authority of the group. The thing of which he seemed to be most proud was his idol house. It was just another thatch roofed shed with a sort of shelf woven out of vines and suspended from the rafters. He forbade us to come closer than about ten feet. On this hanging table there were several half gourds fronted with crudely shaped faces. Of the three larger ones he explained that the greatest was the father and the next in size the mother, and the third their son. All the rest were the "saints." It appears that they feed these gods and saints regularly and with due ceremony by placing in the gourd some of their favorite sweetened foods and anointing their faces therewith. It is probable that they are also used as incense burners.

The Lacondones are entirely self-sufficient, not needing anything from the outside world. They keep a perpetual fire burning by pointing the trunks of three burning logs together in the center of their thatched shelter—thus eliminating the need for matches. Salt is out of their range but they have a salty substance which they obtain from the ashes of a certain palm tree.

As is the case with all Central Americans, corn is their staple food. Corn had its origin with their ancient Mayan ancestors and they still plant it in the same manner. They merely fell a small portion of densely timbered land and burn the timber. Then with a sharpened stick they punch holes and drop in seven grains of corn. That is all. The corn grows about fifteen feet tall and is about matured when the jungle overgrows it.

The men let their hair and beards grow except for cutting bangs in front. The women tie their hair back and adorn it by attaching, at waist level, a piece of skin with the feathers on it from some one of the many colorful birds.

They make their own bows and arrows and hunt with them. They have hardwood arrows, using very distinct forms for both bird and fish shooting. Fragments of broken bottles are now used from which to chip out arrowheads like the ones previously made by the North American Indian from flint. There is an abundance of wild meat; however, the Lacondones do keep some domesticated hogs.

One of the finest hogs I have ever seen in Central America was there. He had been offered in exchange for a bride for the elder son. The father of the girl was willing to the exchange but demanded that the live hog be delivered first. The young man was fearful that the fat hog could not stand the trip in the tropical heat, so was asking for the girl and wanting the proposed in law to come to get his hog.

We were rather surprised to find that these most primitive people seem to appreciate vegetables and care for them even better than their so-called civilized neighbors. Besides the planted foods, they have ready access to the many fruits and edible greens of the forest. Cotton grows almost wild, so they can make their own clothing.

I know of cases in which young Lacondon men have left their primitive homes and lost their identity by changing customs to conform with the Spanish speaking mixed race which now is moving into these jungles. Assimilation is probably the answer to the Lacondon problem.

As we press on to the ends of the earth with the gospel we see men uplifted by its power. One tourist told me seriously that we missionaries are spoiling the world for tourists— if we keep on there won't be any pagans left for the tourists to go to see.

CHAPTER II
Meet Some Native Christians

Though Jauquin (pronounced "Wakeen") speaks and reads Spanish, he is really an Indian. He has been matching the rigors of jungle life so long that he no longer thinks of people as his parents did—as being high class or low class. Out in Peten a man is just what he proves himself to be, no more and no less. Color and class lines have faded out.

Jauquin was left a widower with a large family and when we first met him at church he had with him a young woman dressed in Indian costume. She could not understand all of the message but he certainly told her at home in their dialect what had been said.

With his grown sons, he built a house in town so that the family could be there for the church services over the weekends. During weekdays they lived on their farm, as Indian custom dictated even long before Spanish colonial days. His farm was located at the halfway point in the treacherous jungle trail to Sayaxche. Many times we have rested and eaten at his farm home, and when the trail is very muddy we have sometimes gone on in his little canoe. Often he has taken his mules through the jungles in deep mud to take the messengers of the gospel on their way.

We wear moccasins with leather leggings when the mud is deep. Once when Juaquin was driving his mules for us he took off his moccasins and hung them on a tree, proceeding along barefooted through the mud mingled with roots and stones and thorns.

Juaquin loved God but could not be a member of our church until he married the woman with whom he lived. When at last they obtained their marriage license by going to the governmental center at Flores, they were ready for the marriage. I went out to the church and found three couples awaiting this, their final step in making restitution for their years of sinful living. Juaquin and his wife had butchered and brought a hog and plenty of tamales. They had worked long into the night preparing the food which they brought from their farm. At the close of that day we baptized the three couples and received members into the church. They had been on probation for a long time and I had scolded them and pleaded with them each time I had visited their church. From that day forward they have been victorious Christians, growing in grace.

Not long after his marriage Juaquin passed through some great trials. Malaria ravaged his body at last and he was sick and weak for a long time. He came to me and asked for just enough money to buy a little corn. We seldom lend money to a native because it places an undue hardship on him to pay it back. I gave Juaquin fifty cents and told him to keep it. He declared that he would pay it back and, true to his word, long after I had forgotten it he came with the money.

Then through the connivance of certain malevolent persons he became involved in a property dispute which resulted in his taking the course of Isaac of old, who, when others claimed his wells, went and dug new ones. So Juaquin left the farm that he had dreamed would be a home someday and moved to Subin. Here he built himself a new house of poles and palms and began to urge us to come and hold services, so that his neighbors could hear the gospel preached. The town was so small that I gave it little heed, as we had urgent work to do in larger centers. At last he prevailed on us to stay overnight when passing through and we preached to his neighbors.

He built a larger house especially for a chapel. He decorated all the walls with some old Sundayschool pictures. As we returned from a more remote trip his happy wife met us with hot coffee and they made us rest while he went out to invite his neighbors to service. To our amazement a table was soon spread with great tamales spiced with red peppers till there was not a dry eye at that feast! Having finished eating, we arranged the seats in the chapel. They consisted of boxes, split logs, blocks, gas cans, and benches made from a hewn plank with a hole in each end through which forked sticks were passed to make legs. But all the villagers came! In subsequent services, six new souls were saved in that place.

What a man is this Juaquin! He isn't much for looks but there is boundless energy in that little man of the jungles and he loves God. He built a chapel alone after suffering sickness and great financial reverses. Then he influenced his neighbors to come to church. He sets an example for them in Christian living. He has a son preparing for the ministry now. After the first service in his new chapel, where all his neighbors heard the gospel for the first time, he embraced me and through great sobs tried to express his gratitude for our coming.

I am fully grateful for Juaquin. Having ardent friends like Juaquin takes the sacrifice out of missionary life.

BENANCIO AND LOLA

Benancio and Lola were married two days after the wedding of the former's youngest son. Both of them had been widowed. They had lived together outside of wedlock for many years and had a daughter about ten years old. They had long been persuaded that the gospel was the truth and had sent their children to church and Sunday school. Although they themselves would come occasionally, they had little fellowship and were of no use in the church.

Benancio had been a bad drunkard and was severely addicted to tobacco. When he saw the truth of the gospel he began to seek God's help. Most of the time he was ashamed to enter the church, as he felt condemned for his vices. He would wait till dark and then follow the lake shore around town and then climb the hill and come to church the back way, trying in that manner to keep the villagers from knowing that he was attending the services. Another reason for sneaking to church and listening to the services from the shadows was that he did not care to bring reproach on the church for its having a man in attendance who did not live up to the Christian standards.

He did attend camp meeting, however, and at last he was so moved upon by the Holy Spirit that he came forward and, alter a tremendous struggle in prayer, he was miraculously cured of his perverted appetite for alcohol and nicotine. From that day on, he was out and out for God but still could not be of any service in the church because of his marital status. So when at last the marriage ceremony of Benancio and Lola was completed there was not one bit of condemnation left on their souls. Instead of kissing the bride, Benancio broke out in testifying and Lola followed suit. Never have I heard more impressive testimonies than those two.

Both of them serve on the church board today. They are good tithers and hard workers and enthusiastic in their support of anything that will advance the kingdom of God. Three of his children are entering the Christian ministry.

Lola is a good cook and her house is always open to any servant of God. Benancio is a farmer after the primitive manner of the ancients. He also works some in the chewing gum harvest. Many are the tales he can tell of life in the jungles. He guided me on a threeday trip to visit the little farms in the jungle. He prepared food one night and was an attentive host—though our fare was more primitive than you could imagine. He was the best guide I have ever had, for he was willing to teach me everything. I learned of several fine foods in the jungles.

Though their skin is dark and their food is coarse, they are real Christians, tenderhearted, loving, fearing God. I wouldn't trade their fellowship for a place in royalty.

CHAPTER III
Exploring the Jungle

This is a dream world! There are so many kinds of jungle life that one cannot comprehend it all. An ideal climate for all, yet there is a merciless struggle for existence and a survival of only the fittest. Though it be noon on a bright day, you will see very little sunlight. There are giant trees, but you are hardly aware of them nor can you identify them as to kind. There is a thick undergrowth of ferns and young saplings and thorny vines. Up a little higher your gaze falls upon a maze of vines and parasites, some drooping downward in the shade and others climbing toward a ray of light from above. Orchids and moss are hanging from every available spot. Everything that is strong enough to bear weight has a vine of some kind climbing it. Vines that spiral around a limb will deform it but not kill it.

But here is the vicious love tree. It sprouts from a seed high up in the treetops. At first it grows as a parasite, dropping its "roots" very rapidly toward the earth. They come straight down without a joint for a hundred feet, sometimes looking very much like insulated electric wires. Upon reaching the ground they take root in the soil and shortly they begin to put out twin feelers. Those feelers, which find the trunk of the tree which is already supporting their weight, take hold and root into the tree bark. Such feelers grow thick until they present the fantastic appearance of hugging in a tight embrace. The original vine grows thicker and becomes wood. Soon it shoots out its own tree leaves even above those of the giant tree which supports it. After a few years of such relentless "loving," the supporting tree succumbs and the great lover has fortified itself by its robbery till it grows on above—at last having only a hollow place in the netted trunk where once a good tree stood. The love tree is artificial. It is good for nothing. In fact, its shade keeps a trail muddy and retards the progress of good vegetation.

The jungle is full of wild life as well as insect life. There are many species that are almost unbelievably strange. Contrary to what you may think—it is difficult to get to see wild animals. However, the howler monkeys will follow you by climbing through the treetops. To hear them you would perhaps think that your doom is sealed. If you will sit down quietly they will often come directly overhead to have a closeup look at you.

Of course sitting quietly is not all that one could desire, even though tired, because the cloud of mosquitoes is there the moment one stops. A fast hiker can keep them just one pace behind him.

The narrow trails that exist in the jungles are there in the interest of the chewing gum base. This harvest is carried on in the rainy season, and men and mules muck up the mud until often one drops in knee-deep. Water stands in the tracks and one never knows how far in his foot will go nor what it will strike. It is more a matter of weaving back and forth than walking as one travels in the rainy season. There is a network of roots under the ground. It is amazing what an obstacle is made by a small pole in the road when one is already away below the surface of the earth. If you fall you are quite certain to encounter thorns on either side of the trail.

    For jungle travel it is essential to have good boots or moccasins with leggings. Once I was trekking through the jungle with a young Christian, who is now in Bible school preparing for the ministry. He was wearing high boots and I shoes. He was accustomed to carrying his big loads of chewing gum in similar conditions. We both carried packs. At last he said to me, 'Put your pack on the top of mine and we can go faster." When a chaplain, I often carried my communion set and extra literature, making my army equipment heavier than that of others, but yet I found myself able to help others. However, it is different in the jungle. After much resistance I at last let that little giant take both our loads and I almost had to trot to follow him. His clothing soaked through and perspiration ran off his nose in a stream. I have never in my life been more grateful to a man.

    There is an abundance of snakes in the jungles; but, as with other wild animals who find hiding in the jungle is very easy, it is quite difficult to see them often. The little coral snake is very poisonous, but he is gentle. He is found either in the jungles or in the clearings near one's house—or even in it. The one snake feared above all others is the yellow beard. He ranges from black to green in color and is quite large and always has a yellow throat. The bite of even a small yellow beard makes one spit blood from the lungs, and a large amount of the snake's venom makes blood seep from the pores of one's skin. The only one I have seen in the wild was gracefully crossing the river on which we were traveling by canoe and we were unable to overtake him. This yellow beard is found mostly in the deep jungle, far from the residences of people, but is wild and easily excited and ready to strike at any time. Even so, one person alone is in very little danger. A poisonous snake seldom strikes at the first impulse. It takes several scares to make him strike. A neighbor was bitten when he followed his dogs in a chase for a species of wild pig. As the noisy animals passed by, they provoked the snake and he struck the man coming behind. A lad was bitten as he came away from the pond with his buckets of water. Doubtless he had excited the snake as he neared the pond with his empty buckets.

    Of course we have so many fireflies that they will almost light the town in certain seasons. There is a beetle which has headlights that give a constant bright light of the same color as the light of the fireflies. One can capture about five of these beetles and put them under a drinking glass and have enough light to see to read by. If they are left, the light will dim down; but if they are moved, the light shines again. Children catch these beetles in the month of April and sell them to society ladies. By putting a string about the beetle's abdomen, one can hang it on his lapel and it is very pretty for evening wear. If one is placed in a fresh hollow sugar cane during the day, it can be kept for a long while.

There are several phosphorescent worms, too. The most interesting one is just over an inch long. He has a headlight in front and lights under each of his many legs. If put on a finger on a dark night, it gives much the appearance of a fast passenger train going rapidly over winding tracks with a headlight and lights in all the windows.

RIVERS

One mighty river, the Passion, meanders through the jungles of Peten. Though it is more crooked than a snake, it affords a means of transportation for a wealth of mahogany logs. There are several tributaries and adjacent lakes also. These are full of large fish, turtles, and alligators. Turtles are very good to eat, as are their eggs. Alligator eggs are also sought for human consumption.

A day on the river is an education in itself. Certainly no larger than necessary, the canoe is often so narrow that one cannot stand with his feet crosswise in the bottom. The long paddle that is used has a V shaped "tongue," which is sharpened. Every possible advantage is taken to push on the ground if one is near a shore or in shallow water. Then if one passes under the overhanging foliage he always takes advantage of it for a good shove. It is a matter of highest skill and certainly gives play to excellent teamwork to proceed steadily and quietly with a precious cargo that should not get wet. The cargo could be corn or brown sugar which you are transporting, or it could be a distinguished person.

    All goes well on the big river but the fun begins as we go into a tributary. The entrance is so obscured by the jungle that we would never have imagined that there was a break in the wall of jungle. However, the natives enter it without a word of discussion. Now we make a sharp turn against the current. If we let the current rush us wrong, we are sure to flood the little canoe. Vines hang from overhead, slapping one in the face, and thorns present a sharp warning on every hand. The light grows dim on the brightest day, as now the overgrowth closes in above. The man at the back of the canoe has the responsibility of guiding the craft, and such tricks as he performs you never saw! The paddles work in silence except as the men push hand over hand against some tree limb and, after reaching the end of the long paddle, they let it fall with a mighty slap on the water. These men meet the currents and riffles and obstructions, such as fallen logs, with very little comment. Of course, a machete is always present.

The foliage is of stupendous beauty. Everything demands observation. Here on the edge is a clump of white lilies blooming. Such lovely fragrance! Each of the many thin pistils ends in a sort of T shape but this cross of the T hangs loosely, as if on a swivel.

Overhead are seen various members of the parrot family —the most beautiful being the colorful macaw. Listening, one can sometimes hear the multiplied grunts of a herd of the large and vicious wild hogs called joboli (pronounced "hoboly"). Rounding the bend, one finds where they have been wallowing in the mud. There in the bottom is a stretch of mud where an alligator has just left his smoke screen.

Seldom does one find a place to land; and if one should land there would be no place to go, as the jungle is impenetrable—except by use of a machete.

At last we break out onto a clearing and we pull to shore beside another canoe tied there. We get out and follow a path until we come to a thatch shack and there we find people. How glad they are to see us! The lady fixes us some tortillas and fries some turtle eggs and perhaps even has some boiled fish or monkey or wild turkey, and we eat heartily without any formalities or equipment. We speak a few words about our wonderful Savior and the workmen play a practical joke or two, and then we press on.

Then a strange noise which sounds like voices in the distance makes us ask if we are nearing a village. No, no, if so we would hear a dog or a rooster. What and where is that sound heard away over yonder? Oh! That is a mischievous kind of frog that clings to the bottom of the boat and sings over the joy of his hitchhiking success.

It used to be that the good natives would have me sit down in a canoe while they carried me as a precious cargo. I would arrive as stiff as a board. Now I demand a paddle and try my hand at every trick of the game. If the rivers were not so crooked they would afford a good way to travel. Sometimes when the waters are high one can cut out many of the river bends, and in such time it certainly is better to go by water than to wade the mud in the trail over the land.

CHAPTER IV
Going Native

Let's eat with the natives. Help yourself! Almost all the food that comes to the table has been cooked and if you are hungry it will do you good. These tortillas (pronounce ll as if it were y) are the principal food. They are the size of pancakes, but thin and white. They are patted out by hand from dough made of soaked corn ground wet. No flavor! Though a hungry native can eat fifteen of them, an average missionary rebels with the fourth one. Yet our metabolism is such as to require a third more calories than the natives eat!

The table is generally so low that one can't get his knees under it, or it may be so tall that one needs to stand up to eat from it. For us, they have spread a cloth on the table and have bought some new enameled dishes from a little store that sells them. The wash pan now contains the chicken soup. (You washed your hands in it just five minutes ago.) There may be a spoon for you but no fork and knife and no tableware for the man of the house. Most likely your spoon was in use in the kitchen when you started to eat and the lady comes wiping it on her dirty apron, then running her thumb over it to be sure it is clean.

Coffee is made just the right temperature to drink by boiling and then cooling by pouring it from one half gourd to another. Just before serving it to visitors, the good lady turns her back and tastes it. Once when my family was with me our boy Earl Dean, Jr., failed to close his eyes as we asked the blessing and as we began to eat he was weeping; through his sobs he declared in English that the old lady had gotten her germs in the coffee.

    Seldom will the men of the family eat with you and you never see the women and children eating. They do not know how to eat at a table. The mother eats over the fire as she cooks, and the children are given a plate or half gourd of food and they squat on the dirt floor as they eat. I had a sixteen year old youth eat in our home with me one day and he sat away back from the table. He was helpless in trying to use a fork. I could see no bread at his plate, so I offered him some. He declared he had some and at last I discovered that he was holding it down by his lap—breaking pieces from it as he ate.

    There will invariably be several hungry dogs gazing upon you so fixedly that you can see to a depth of several hungry generations in their eyes. It's proper to toss them the bones. Little children too will watch the special foods as you consume them, hoping earnestly that you will leave a morsel. Often the doors and windows are filled with children watching to see how the foreigner eats.

    The chickens have been called out of the house as a special courtesy to you, but surely while we eat some good old hen will come in quietly to lay! Also some adventuresome young chicks will be in to see if some crumb has fallen from the table.

This chicken soup is for this one very special occasion but black beans will be the daily fare. If they are boiled there is bean soup, too. The natives love to pour pork lard over their boiled beans on their plates. Then sometimes the beans are ground and served in a thick, puddinglike texture. Then they are considered best of all when they are ground and fried in plenty of lard till they are sort of French fried and molded into a large bean weighing about two pounds or more.

Fruit and vegetables are never placed on the table. In the native mind, you come to the table to eat "food." However, you are often offered a grapefruit or an avocado or even a boiled sweet potato between meals. Always before leaving the table you say, "Thank you very much," to each one at the table and the people likewise thank you.

Doubtless I eat with the natives as much as any missionary ever does. I never take provisions as I travel among them. They appreciate this gesture of confidence and seldom will take pay for their food and hospitality. It is always a treat to get back to the mission and eat some of my wife's cooking!

Church officials and often missionaries are fearful of native food. Their fears are entirely unfounded, and if harm befalls them it is usually the fears and not the food that did the damage.

Of course it is difficult to imagine any Americans ever fully adjusting to the shock of a filthy, smoky, dirt floored kitchen, where the food is cooked over an open fire and has the flavor of smoke. Furthermore the native diet just does not have the caloric content to keep up our bodily energy, so one must either supplement his diet or shorten his visits with the natives.

STAYING OVERNIGHT

How shall we ever get ready for bed in this room where everyone else plans to sleep? That is your individual problem! Adult natives never undress openly for night. They may just rest in their hammocks till the others are asleep. Some may rarely sleep with their day clothes on. But most likely they get your attention diverted. And next time you notice they are all wrapped in their sheet for the night.

The natives of the jungles keep a light burning all night. They can turn a kerosene torch down to the smallest spark. Some places they use pitch torches or candles. The custom of burning a light at night is handed down from days when they lived in the open and kept up a fire to frighten the wild animals away. Still, it is a comfort to have a light in case the vampire bats get rabies or in case the army ants decide to establish a united attack on your bedroom or just in case you should have trouble with a scorpion, lizard, frog, spider, or mouse in the night.

Invariably the house must be shut up tight for the night. Since the houses are built without hardware, door props are always used. These are invariably made of some strong, heavy wood and a bit longer than a machete (long native knife) and are useful for defense or for breaking up a knife fight. Of course the thatched roof allows some small amount of ventilation. Night air is considered very harmful and dangerous.

Once when one of our elderly native preachers was sick I visited him and had prayer with him. After I prayed he followed in prayer. He had a bad cold and prayed, "Lord, forgive me now. You know it is my own fault that I'm sick because I opened the window in the night and the air struck me." He recovered and is strong today.

The mystery to me is how they know when it is daylight with the house closed so tight; but they are early risers and almost always are up and dressed and oft times bathed before daylight breaks. There are always roosters to crow, of course, but I really think that it is the discomfort of their sleeping conditions that accounts for early rising. Experience has long since taught me that the body rests much more rapidly and the vigor regained lasts much longer when one sleeps on a solid bed, be it a floor, table, church bench, a board, or a canvas cot.

CHAPTER V
Forming a Church

Visiting a village one Sunday morning, I asked our good native brother who was in charge to go ahead with his Sunday school very much as usual and then I offered to bring them a devotional message at the close. He had some fine children, so he ordered the girls to sing something. From where they sat, they directed the singing. After prayer we began the lesson study with everybody in one class. The good teacher "reads spelling and spells reading." If he could get a few words connected together so as to remind him of something he knew, he could expound the scriptures quite elaborately. But so often the portion of a phrase that he would connect had nothing at all to do with the thoughts of the lessons. However, I must admit that he was teaching them how to live the Christian life.

The people come to church reverently and upon arrival they bow their heads for a silent prayer. Silence and reverence reign till opening time. Many come very early and read their Bibles there in the sanctuary of the little thatched church. One day a little lad of about ten years accompanied my family to church. We had gone by canoe to the Flores church in the island town. Abelino was an Indian boy and had never even gone to school and certainly had never been to church. Of course, he did not know to remove his hat. The superintendent for this Sunday school was an old, retired schoolteacher who had remained fastidious. Upon seeing this humble lad with his homemade straw hat on, the old man tried to remove it for him without disturbing the silence of this quiet period before the service. Abelino managed to keep his hat rather well in position, in spite of the old man's jerks at it, and at last with his hat well planted to his head the little fellow stalked out of the building. Seeing the situation, I went out after the little fellow. He was a stranger on this big island and knew no place to go, so I found him just outside the door. I asked what had gone wrong. He replied that the old man was trying to pull his hair! I explained that the hat was the difficulty, so he gave it to me at my request and we hung it up until after the service. Abelino has continued to attend church and recently he was saved and now his stepfather has also found God.

    This old gentleman teacher held Sunday school for two solid hours, commenting on every sentence of the comments in the quarterly. He was the ablest of them all and they seemed to base their preaching merit on the length of time occupied. They desired services every night of the week and it was impossible to distinguish prayer meeting from Sunday school or devotional or young people's services. All were alike —evangelistic.

Also, I found almost as many backsliders as believers. The good people are ready and willing to evangelize their neighbors and they all love to get together to form an evangelistic expedition. Naturally, some could not go along, and they were considered rather disinterested. They were left behind for many weeks without Christian instruction or communion. After the big tours, those who stayed behind were often found backslidden or at least out of fellowship.

Some of the old-timers had been having their own way for so long and were so set against any change that we had to use very firm authority to instill any new methods, such as division of the Sunday schools into classes, the reception of the tithe during devotional services, and the distinguishing of church members from Sunday school members. By God's help we won; and anyone who visits these churches today will see that they function nicely and profitably, helping already with more than half the support of their native preachers. Many backsliders have returned to God and many others are on the verge of seeking His pardon. Best of all, we have an organization into which we can fit the new converts with reasonable hope for their edification.

In multiplied cases we get the interest of a family—perhaps by means of the medical work or in some other way. Soon the man attends church and finds to his surprise that he is welcomed. Soon he brings his wife and at last his children. If they attend church it isn't long until they get under conviction and seek God and become happy finders. As the children come to the age of responsibility they too find God. Of course, the parents have probably been living together by common consent rather than by marriage and, before we can receive them into church membership or dedicate their infants, they must be married.

Parliamentary procedure is entirely foreign to them, too. It is amusing and somewhat tedious to conduct democratic church meetings in a new church. Some who are still on probation because they do not yet fully qualify for church membership always want to vote and talk. Then, if we must vote by ballot, those who do not know how to write will seldom assert their authority in telling the scribe what to write on a ballot! So the scribe wins the election.

In some places I have not been able to provoke a discussion. I find that the ancient Indian customs prevail. If one does "stick his neck out" and discuss a matter, he is certainly in bad repute when the natives get together outside the meeting. In certain places I have to call a church meeting and lay out my proposition and then dismiss the group. Next meeting one will be prepared to speak the opinion of the group and then we can vote. Of course we are breaking down this custom as they find that it is safe to be democratic.

CHAPTER VI
Healing the Sick

NATIVE TREATMENTS

With the wealth of vegetation it is understandable that the Guatemalans discovered the medical content of certain herbs. One particular herb from which natives make tea is a very effective stimulant to milk giving on the part of mothers with nursing infants. But for the most part their "cures" are absurd and even cruel and unsanitary. Any lady there who has reared a family and has tried to be helpful to her neighbors in times of sickness will be able to tell you a home remedy for every possible sickness. She can recite to you the formulas as easily as our mothers can tell how to make biscuits. To cure the flu you need some coyote manure. It must be thoroughly dried and then toasted and at last finely ground and sprinkled into the patient's porridge.

Never have I gone to the bedside of a gravely sick person without finding some kind of herbs bound to his body. To cure skin diseases they know of plants that will burn the skin very severely, and often they come to us for medical help in such horrible conditions as a result of their primitive treatments that it is very difficult to discover what the original symptoms were. A jaw swollen from an ulcerated tooth is often pierced many times with a long thorn to let the soreness out. If one has pleurisy pains it is believed that the night air has hit him. For relief one must first find some way to suck out that air himself. One way to do it is to soak a ball of cotton in liquor and set it on fire. While burning, it is placed in a drinking glass, the mouth of which covers the bare skin over the painful area. The vacuum left from the oxygen consumption pulls the flesh into the glass nicely and then the area is massaged with this form of suction cup. If a few treatments of that do not give relief, the natives must look for the rarest type of long thorn which is hollow. With that, the soreness is let out of the pleural cavity.

    They have health precautions that are adhered to more strictly than our American precaution of avoiding getting wet feet. The native who bathes must always wet his head or it will cause great damage in sickness or even insanity. In places where the people can get to the rivers and lakes, they bathe frequently. Only one other kind of bath is recognized: that is, taking a big bucket of water and a gourd and while standing pouring the water on the head, letting it run over the body. Bars of laundry soap are used generously for bathing. A traveler who asks for a bath will be brought a bucket of water and the living room is his. They are delighted to have you wet down the floor. Baths in public hospitals are unheard of. Our "cat baths" with a washcloth and a pan of water could never be called a bath in their language.

    Another health precaution almost religiously observed is not to expose one's self to the cool air if one is warm. A lady will do her ironing with a charcoal filled flatiron with the house shut up tight so that the air cannot strike her. She cannot go to church in the evening after cooking or ironing. And certainly one does not bathe that same day.

  I installed hot water in the kitchen sink and it takes considerable time to get a hired girl to use hot and cold water interchangeably without fear. Since they are accustomed to cooking over a little open flame, they have great fear of our stoves. The parents of one of the girls that worked in a mission home tried to get the missionaries to erect a brick wall in front of the stove, as they were sure that the heat and cold would presently damage her internally.

  All foods and medicines are classified as either "hot" or "cold." Pork meat is hot; beef is cool. Most fruit juices are cool. I was eating delicious tree ripened grapefruit one day and offered some to a companion. He declined, explaining that he had a cold and for that reason could certainly eat nothing so cool, though he likes grapefruit very much.

  The average infant mortality is 50 per cent. That is to say that half the children die before they are two years of age. As soon as they are able to crawl they infect themselves with the intestinal worms that are prevalent everywhere. Living as they do on dirt floors and so little above the status of beasts, there is no escape until they have a change of heart that will change their outlook and their desires. Then, too, most of the people have malaria either in active or dormant form. When malaria is active it leaves a person very anemic after an attack. If it remains dormant it ruins one's liver and spleen. One of the most popular surgical operations in Central America is the removal of great portions of overgrown livers.

Even tiny infants have no escape from malaria. While malaria is tricky to identify when it has been beaten around by prophylactic dosages, it is as plain as a book in its natural form. But malaria is not so prevalent as it is often supposed. The most common cause of the general anemia comes from intestinal worms. There is everything from amoeba to tapeworms a yard long. The sure sign of worms in children is their protruding abdomens. With adults more frequently one finds sores that will not heal and of course a pale complexion. From malnutrition, malaria, and internal parasites, the people, particularly the children, are so weakened that they readily succumb to the many communicable diseases which know no quarantine.

The most common treatment we give is the worm purge. This problem of combating worms becomes so acute at times that I know of cases when drastic measures have been taken in attempting to gain relief. Sometimes a child falls into a delirious state with twitching muscles and gnashing teeth. Not long ago my wife was frantically summoned to the bedside of a little girl about eight years old. Mint leaves had been packed around the unconscious little one and a generous amount of laundry bluing had been used on the leaves. Symptoms were quite clear. The girl was poisoned from the toxin the worms throw off. With first aid measures my wife was able to restore that little one. Afterwards more effective treatment was given. The mothers will often claim that they gave the child treatment but inquiry reveals that perhaps they used methods that are terribly irritating, often leaving the child screaming from pain.

There is an ancient and primitive worm killer. I am convinced that it would work—perhaps killing more than just the worms! It is a concoction made from a weed that I must describe as having a hundred times the stinging force of nettles. The most unbearable torture I have ever suffered was when I got into a patch of them. From a previous contact with one just touching my arm I had found that continuous washing in water would relieve the unbearable smarting. But when I walked through a great patch of them in the bushes and found both my arms and legs on fire there was no water available. I couldn't stand it! Once while I was wading in water a spider got inside my trousers and stung me severely. That too makes a hot spot but, its being concentrated in one spot, I bore it till I could find a bit more favorable place to treat myself. But when this nettle sets one on fire all over, there is nothing in the world like it. The worm purge is made from the fuzz or the actual stingers of these nettles mixed into a sweetened drink. Some grind egg shells into a fine power and make a drink that is reputed to be helpful.

MISSIONARY MEDICAL TREATMENTS

Mrs. Hunter has been helping her neighbors with all their ailments. Here are a few cases. A lady borrowed her husband's machete to cut something about the kitchen but she split her thumb. Bleeding could not be stopped, as they did not know how to use a tourniquet. She was a day's journey by mule back from the village. They tried one home remedy after another, packing the thumb in lime, then in mud, then in manure. They wrapped it with bandage strips, but the blood continued to flow. At last the husband saddled his mules and, bringing along some eggs for market, they began to rush the wounded lady to our little clinic. Shortly she had lost so much blood that she could ride no more, so he helped her from the horse and laid her on the ground. As she seemed to be dying, he thought of his eggs. He broke fresh eggs into her mouth and she revived and shortly was able to continue a little farther. Three times she had to be treated in this manner and by the time she arrived the bleeding had ceased.

The lime and other concoctions had burned the skin on her entire hand and proud flesh had set in on the thumb. It was about the ugliest little wound I have ever seen and it seemed that she would be left at best with a deformed thumb, as it was split through the nail. Mrs. Hunter cleaned that hand and dressed it daily for several weeks, and today the thumb is well shaped, though of course it has a great scar.

Another lady rushed up to our house with a bleeding hand. All five fingers were lacerated and we found that in a knife fight she had grabbed the blade of a sharp knife. At first she said she was cutting meat in her kitchen when the knife slipped. Later, however, the facts were revealed.

Very often they will hide their real symptoms, seeming to feel that they are going to just test the ability of their nurse in discerning the ailment. Sometimes they even lie. But one day an incident occurred that has offered us many a laugh. A man arrived with a finger mashed and lacerated. His common-law wife was with him. Mrs. Hunter started to clean and dress the finger and of course inquired as to how such a severe wound could occur. He broke out crying in great, heavy sobs there in the presence of his wife and revealed that she had bitten him in a fight they were having.

One young man came in with a toothache and wanted the tooth pulled. Mrs. Hunter said that she would never have the strength in her hands to pull his molar but suggested that her husband could. The tooth looked to me as if it could be saved if there were a dentist to fill it, but there was none. The man could not afford to buy a ticket on the airplane to go out to where a dentist is. He said the pain was unbearable and that he had dug at it so much that he had it loose already and that if he had just a little pull on it he could be rid of it. At last I told him to come the next day if he couldn't stand it any longer. Early in the morning he was there. He sat down and I took a firm hold of that tooth with the forceps and tried to loosen it. It was absolutely solid and I found that I had to hold his head with one hand, as I was dragging him. I rested and told him that he should really try to save the tooth. It was hollow, though, and possibly beyond repair. As he had taken nothing to deaden the pain, he now had great tears in his eyes. He said, "You just don't have the nerve to pull it." Finally, I pulled the tooth out.

    As is so often the case, Mrs. Hunter was frantically called to a home where they said a baby was dying. It had whooping cough and was strangling to death. She simply had the mother reach her finger down its little throat and grab out the phlegm and the little one began to get its breath and lived.

    One rare case was that of a man who fell into the crotch of a large tree, wedging his leg just above the knee. He hung there head downward for twenty-two hours and in desperation, after cutting one fork of the tree and not getting it to fall, he tried to cut his leg off at the thigh.

    I stumbled onto my young people's president one day in a maimed condition. In his attempt to fell a large dead tree, a large limb had fallen on his shoulder and left him unconscious for a day or more. When he regained consciousness, his family took him to an old quack doctor, who had proved able in many cases of bone setting. This shoulder was not only out of place, but shattered, and a nerve was pinched, causing immobility of the arm. The doctor prescribed tea made of avocado leaves and castor oil to be taken internally. He set the joint in place but it would never stay, due to the fracture, I suppose. By the time I made them realize there would be no benefits from these manipulations it was too late for effective treatment. Since then he has gone to the best of doctors and they give him no hope of ever using his arm again.

CHAPTER VII
Comforting the Bereaved

Returning home in the canoe one Sunday morning, my family was attracted by a loud shouting to the scene of a drowning. A family from out in the meadow country was visiting here in the lake city and the boys had gone bathing. The younger lad, being about twelve, did not know how to swim but was fearless. At last his older brother told him to stay in the canoe while he took a swim to a little distance away. When no one was close by, the lad shouted and jumped in and before others could reach him he was resting quietly on the shallow bottom of the clear lake. They brought him up but were fearful that he was dead. They were able to feel his heart beating still. Then they suddenly remembered that the law says that one is not to touch a dead person till the officers of the law are called, so they let him fall back into the water. Of course when they drew out the body again much later it was too late. Never have I faced a more impossible situation in trying to offer consolation.

A neighbor of mine, who was quite a drunkard, had talked with me and we were trying to get his legal papers fixed so he could honor his wife and six children by proper marriage. He seemed to be trusting in God and walking in the light. As he left home for the long season of work in the jungles to care for the pack mules of a large chewing gum contracting company, he came over to see me and we had prayer together and he recommended his family to my care.

One day word filtered through the school that our neighbor Filipe was killed. After trying to verify the rumors, the good woman went directly to the man who leads the company and asked him pointblank. He turned pale and fabricated a story. He said, "Yes, your husband is very ill and we have sent out to bring him in." Upon her departure from his office he called in a neighbor and asked him to fabricate another story for the "truth" to tell her. He came and told me the false story. We brought in this stricken neighbor lady and together told her that the truth was that her husband was dead and had been found lying peacefully still, holding the bridle of his horse. The ungodly man went on to "console" her by saying that it was certainly the will of God. Later that day I learned the truth that a bandit had shot from behind close ambush and that very moment an inspecting party had just returned with their report of how they had covered his maggot infested body. The bandit had escaped with all the six mules and their packs as well as the good saddle pony.

Poor woman and children! Although the man always drank up all he had earned and was often away from home, his death left its mark anyway. It was truly a comfort to me to know that Filipe had just begun to walk in all the light he had when I had last seen him.

One afternoon when my wife was out making her rounds of sick calls in the home and I was doing some work with the jeep, some ladies beckoned me frantically and I followed them into a half constructed mud hut. There in a hammock lay a dying infant. Its eyes were set and it was gasping for breath. Strong little heart and lungs would not give up. I recalled that my own boy had been in an oxygen tent once when I was far from him in the war—otherwise his fate would have been just as this child's. Down there they have bottled oxygen to put the fizz in the soda pop, but no one but us has ever dreamed of needing it to spare the life of a dying infant. I tried to get them to bundle up this little one and let me take it to the so called hospital. But as they say they had "abandoned it to death" and they stood there and watched it die. I could do nothing more but breathe a prayer and it seemed that God did the best for this innocent, illegitimate infant of an abandoned girl. That night I went back to see if I could offer some consolation. I slipped in almost unnoticed, as they had plenty of liquor and playing cards and the candles burned bright at the feet of the little body, lighting the dingy room to a degree of hilarity that had never been known there before. They had cut down a cardboard carton to make the box for the body and had papered it with pretty colors. That Indian girl mother sat squatted on the floor with a sister that was with her. One fellow who could interpret my thoughts gave them a few quiet words of consolation, and I left that house in its hilarious debauchery for the night. The next day I saw them take the little box to the cemetery.

When death occurs, the law allows twenty-four hours' maximum time till the burial must be completed. Certainly the putrefaction that sets in encourages such. There are no undertakers and a carpenter is sought the first thing. He generally is late arriving with the box. The body must be lifted from the table and placed in the box and the lid nailed down. It is hard work bearing the box on the shoulders of four men in the heat of the tropics. The cemeteries are far out too. Arriving at the cemetery they try to lower the box into the grave, only to find the latter too small. Then someone gets in and digs a little and other attempts are made.

There is something of a relaxation after burying one's own dead, which I observe is wholesome. We are missing that in America when we so far remove ourselves from the presence of death—and the shock of reality finds us unprepared.

CHAPTER VIII
Introducing Native Pastors

ISIDRO

Isidro's boyhood was rugged and rigorous. He is very small but, as someone said of him, he is *pura essencia*. The idea comes from the custom of making essence of coffee, for in it you have a lot of the real thing in a very small package. We sent Isidro and his family out to Poptun to establish a church in a new town that was springing up around a new airstrip. When we first visited him, he was living in a dirt floored hut, twelve by sixteen feet. He had screened off one end for his bedroom and was having as many as thirty in attendance in the services held in the rest of the house. To Isidro, however, the house is never too crowded. In addition to his family of six, I recall having slept with seven others in that little house.

Isidro is a soul winner; many of our outstanding Christians can tell of their first contact with the gospel when they talked to Isidro in the road somewhere.

He is carefree and no hardship or rebuff will long dampen his spirits. I have been in travels with him when our food was anything but satisfactory, but he didn't complain. One night he arranged a bed for me; then he lay down on some sacks and slept with his clothes on.

His first religious feelings were negative, as his family tried to force him to kiss an idol. However, when he first heard the gospel story, with its living God of love, there was a positive response in his soul which has never waned. Upon the completion of his Bible school work, God gave him a fine wife and they have five sweet children today. Since they have lost only two, they are above the average. They have served in several pastorates but this one in Poptun has tried their mettle and proved them good. Food prices were so inflated out there that they could in no way have fruit or vegetables to eat.

With mission funds we helped them build a modest church building. As they were so remotely situated and no funds were available for air transportation, at one time two years slipped by without my paying them a visit. When I did pay them a visit, I found them discouraged but still trying. Only about eleven attended the church services but we called on several other families and urged them to get saved. In a few weeks Isidro wrote me that he was having a spontaneous revival. Shortly he invited us to come and organize the congregation into a church and we did with forty-two charter members. In a few months they rebuilt their building and there were many other signs of healthy growth.

Today, Isidro, having started in Poptun with nothing, is pastoring one of our best churches in Guatemala. He has a vision for starting the work in about sixteen outlying villages. Do pray for him.

RAQUEL

Raquel is a woman of prayer, and she has a keen understanding of people. She is about the best altar worker we have in Guatemala. My first knowledge of her was in seeing her praying and weeping and instructing seekers. She is a good pastor, too, and is quick to direct the conversation to the interests of the kingdom of Heaven. She is neat and pretty with fair skin and straight black hair. She was well trained in our Nazarene Bible school in Coban, and after graduation she stayed on at the school for several years in a responsible position.

At last we placed her as pastor in a remote village where the people were deplorably ignorant, sickly, and superstitious. She lived with another young lady for a companion, and it was not long until they were able to perfect a church organization. They worked against great odds but were constantly victorious. They visited outlying villages too and now have several converts attending from two of these villages.

I am confident that Raquel can preach, but when we visit her church she takes a very retiring place. First she serves us lemonade and fruits and then begins the preparation of the food. All the while she makes the most of her opportunity to talk over the problems and victories of her ministry.

Upon visiting her church on one occasion, I asked her if she would like us to help her with some pastoral calls, as we had some time before the service. She was glad for the help and took us to three places where she had visited before and felt she needed help. First was a wealthy Catholic home where there was sickness and a need. We left the idolatry of Catholicism pretty well in ruins in that home.

Then we visited an old lady who also was not a Christian but she had seen a vision, or as they say she had experienced a revelation, and was ready for Christian instruction. After she told me of her revelation, I read some portions of the prophecies of Jesus to her from my Bible and she exclaimed, "That is it! That's exactly what I saw! Read it again, please!" How great is our God to try to enlighten a benighted soul!

Lastly, we went to the home of a lady who had heard the gospel preached in childhood and was in favor of it but, due to great opposition and at last loss of contact with Christian people, she was now married to a drunken owner of a saloon and had a large family. Today that lady is a member of our church, all of her children are Christians, and her husband is attending occasionally.

Good native pastors like Raquel are the best guarantee of the growth and perpetuation of the church work which is now well established. Pray for Raquel.

ARNOLDO

A cartoonist could best depict Arnoldo in the act of dehorning the devil. I heard him declare from the pulpit that he intends to leave the devil with at least one less horn as a result of his ministry. Still, he is a fearful man. In spite of his fine sense of humor, he takes his work and his problems very seriously.

He first heard the gospel when as a lad he had learned to read and a tract fell into the hands of someone in the neighborhood. His illiterate father had him read it and other subsequent tracts to many illiterate neighbors. After the family was saved, Arnoldo at last entered the Nazarene Bible School to prepare for the ministry, feeling a very definite call of God.

But, being as yet unsanctified, he yielded to the sins of the flesh and a moment of sin brought years of dire consequences. Genuine repentance and the grace of God at last restored the man and he was one day permitted to finish his ministerial studies.

While still single, we placed him in the pastorate of a very difficult church. He took such poor material as he found to work with in that church and soon brought order out of chaos.

At last God gave him a fine wife, who is just the kind of quiet and able companion he needs. She, too, has attended our Bible School.

Arnoldo is the best pulpiteer among our native preachers. He is eloquent and inspirational and can feel the response of his audience. He is faithful and fearless in his presentation of truth.

He is the most industrious national I have ever known. No task is too menial for him to do and yet he carries the dignity of a minister of God. He wins friends and wins souls. He is up every morning at daylight and oft times I have called on him late at night, never to catch him asleep.

He is a student and scholar. He has taken a theological course by correspondence since he has been in the pastorate and reads very broadly. He is working hard to learn English so that he can read holiness literature, as there is a poverty of it in the Spanish language. He is loyal to Christ, loyal to our church, and loyal to his missionaries. He should make an outstanding leader in our Guatemala church.

ALFONSO

Alfonso is a timid soul. In Bible school days they nicknamed him "No, Thank You." He off times passed the food to others in the dining hall and remained hungry. I discovered that he spent a whole year without a bed for himself in the parsonage just because he would not admit the need to anyone.

He would never go through a door before me. Once when we were in an evangelistic campaign together and sharing the work and food equally, he still made me go first. I threatened to duck him in the wash pan one day and thus made him wash first. That seemed to break the tension.

He grew up undisciplined and neglected. By the time he was eight years old he could play the marimba so well that they would stand him on a soapbox to play his position at the high notes. Often four or even five players preside at the same marimba.

Marimba music is almost synonymous with dancing and drunkenness and the rest of the degradation that accompanies such diversions. Alfonso had an obsession for music. The dancing sometimes begins shortly after midnight and lasts for more than twenty four hours. He never left the music either for food or rest. By the time Alfonso was eighteen years old he was ruined in health, and his spirit was broken. He testified that he had participated in all manner of sin and found it all bitter. He says that he felt himself as an old man without hope of living more than one more year.

Then the gospel was preached in his hearing. He walked in the first ray of light and has never broken fellowship with God. A little missionary lady took him to the Bible school to enroll him there. The school officials frankly said that they could see no promise in such an unlikely looking chap. But at the insistence of one missionary he was given a try; and he made good! God gave him a splendid wife—one of our Bible school girls.

He has served as pastor in some of our most difficult places and has had remarkable success. Today he is pastoring a church that he has brought from a chaotic state into a perfectly organized and smoothly functioning Church of the Nazarene. He is cooperative with the district program though ever so remote from the center. He has all the auxiliary organizations working well. He invents his own Sunday school contests, and he gets his people to pray and fast, and together they are winning many souls; and he can now bring heaven and earth together with music. He has written several stirring gospel choruses, and how the people love to sing them!

ANATOLIO

Everyone calls him Don Nato for short. He is a grandfather but not an old man. Having lost his first wife, he at last married a young widow woman who is a Christian—so now Don Nato is rearing another family of his own. His younger children are younger than several of his grandchildren.

When I came to know Don Nato he was a faithful layman. He was very quiet but enthusiastic about his religion. He had been saved from a hard, rigorous, sinful life. He was serving as treasurer for our San Benito church and would sometimes fill the pulpit for the pastor. It became clear that he had a call to the ministry and we placed him as pastor of our newly organized church at Sayaxche. That is a backward place and many were his problems and great are the sacrifices he and his family have made to live out there.

Before long, he made the great pastoral achievement of getting three common-law families of new converts married. He has labored faithfully as a pastor. He is a good evangelist. He has had to plant some corn to make ends meet financially, and he worked hard to build a parsonage and kitchen on the church property.

Since he has had no formal education at all, his sermon preparation must be very laborious. However, he is a remarkably good preacher and I know that he is faithful to study and pray. He writes me often. This church is so remote that I cannot often visit it. Always there is a note of victory in his letters and he invariably says that they have the devil stirred up. They must be resisting the devil in a scriptural manner!

Once, his letter said that the whole family was sick with the malaria and bad colds. My good wife prepared a package of medicines and instructions and we sent it to them posthaste by mule back. Next time I saw them they were well, but I found that the sickness had been so severe that all of them were bedfast at one time and when the medicines arrived they took double the prescribed dosages. They felt that, if a little was good, more would be better and furthermore they thought that their sickness was so far advanced that it needed drastic action. Whole pills of atebrin were pushed down the throat of the baby, so weak it was about to die. Such treatment mixed with prayer and faith had the desired effect.

These people not only love their missionaries but out in Sayaxche they esteem them more highly than the greatest political and military leaders of the world. The attitudes of a church reflect the attitudes of its pastor.

CHAPTER X
Four Great Needs

In Jesus' parable of the Great Supper as recorded in Luke 14:16-25 we find four kinds of handicapped, underprivileged people: the poor, the maimed, the halt, and the blind. Since this scripture has a missionary emphasis, we shall use these four conditions as an outline for this missionary message.

Most of what we will describe here is applicable to the greater part of the Latin world. Perhaps it should be more clearly observed that these conditions are almost universally existent where the Roman Catholic Church has had control of the people, both in Europe and in the Americas.

THE POOR

We Americans are the rich people of the world. For one entering America from any other country, it is actually humorous to hear individual Americans complaining about their personal economic struggles. Those who complain the most are the ones that have every gadget and are already expecting to purchase next year's model as soon as it is available! We Americans are poor because we want so much. The contrast is seen in people who don't want anything! They lack aspiration. That is real poverty! One can give a fellow like that wealth and he will soon be poor again. Something must be done for him that goes deeper and touches his desires and his basic concepts of life.

The Latin world is romantic. That means that it lacks our practicality. One result is that manufacturers and merchants do not dream of making modern conveniences available to everybody, as is done in North America. Fine things are thought to be for the wealthy only and even the wealthy have a miserable idea of things.

Missionary William Sedat observes that most of the people for whom he is spending his life possess fewer personal effects in their homes for their lifetime existence than we require for one single night's camping away from home. In fact, if a family needs to move, it is no trouble. All they have in the home worth moving can be carried in one load on their backs in burlap sacks. One of my native preachers comments that the trouble is that such people do not expect to live all of their lives, hence the hand-to-mouth existence!

You have heard of the lethargy "south of the border." It exists! The hammock pictures itself in my memory as a symbol of their poverty. Traveling along the roads of Central America, you are sure to see a man in mid afternoon, when plenty of work could be done, sleeping soundly in his hammock. He is barefooted, never having worn shoes. The shack is unfinished and now so old that it will soon fall down. My observation after using a hammock is that one can never get rested in one. Rest in a hammock calls for more rest immediately.

Added to lethargy is a passionate love for diversions. This results in an almost constant round of festivals and fairs throughout the year. The republic of Guatemala has hardly a week left in the year without an official holiday. They include in their calendar not only their own independence day but that of the United States and that of France and others. Birthdays are elegantly celebrated, as are weddings. There is always a fiesta for some patron saint of some city or town.

The Central American can work hard if he can be motivated to do so. In caring for their families, the women work much more constantly than the men. The fact remains, however, that they do very little work. I hired two men to saw lumber. They collected pay for a week's work and did not work the following week. Then they worked a few days more and collected their bit of pay and never returned. They always tell you that the wage you pay them is not enough to live on, and yet they can lay off at will and hardly turn a hand for weeks and even months without earning a cent. They must hibernate!

In trying to teach the people to be more industrious I scold them and tell them that they like to work three days and then rest for three months. We teach them that the fourth commandment says, "Six days shalt thou labor." Then strict Sabbath observance will give us the proper proportion of rest.

It is beautiful to see how some of our Christian people are being lifted from their old poverty. Here is Juan. He was little better than a bum until after God saved him. Today he supports his large family well and is getting ahead financially. He gets up early every morning and works hard. Best of all, he brings his tithe to God's house on Sunday. God can prosper him that way.

Then there is little Zoila, the hired girl, who was trained to help in our home in order that my wife could devote more time to missionary nursing. Before going to the field some told us that there would be no use to take a washing machine because the native girls could do the laundry and they could not be expected to use the machine. However, Zoila uses it as well as any American woman can. And she likes it! Furthermore, it affords a great economy on soap, clothing, and hired help. Zoila can cook a good meal too and will have it ready when we come in from our varied duties. She has not only learned to work and enjoy it but has learned to save her money and care for her belongings. These natives can be lifted!

In these days when our country has shown so much interest in the underprivileged people of the earth, it is well to observe that the power of the gospel is the only thing that will really raise their economic status. I saw military occupation in Italy make beggars out of many hundreds of people. They met the troop trains to beg cigarettes or bread or coffee from the GI's when they could have been profitably at work in their fields. Going to the mission field through

Mexico, one of the missionaries who was seeing poverty for her first time wept over the poor ones—naked and hungry. I reminded her that a tip given them would be spent tomorrow and a crust of bread would hold them only until night. We must have something better to give, as had Peter and John that day they met the lame beggar on the way to prayer meeting. That poor fellow never needed to beg again. The cause of his poverty was removed in the name of Jesus Christ. I have seen large amounts of money spent on the backward peoples, only to leave them more perverted and poorer. A little money spent through foreign missions will actually lift the needy in this present world, and it will surely be well invested in the light of eternity. This is our answer to communism.

THE MAIMED

Let us observe the intellectual status of the people. Certainly they are so handicapped that they are maimed because of their illiteracy. In most parts of Latin America the proportions of illiteracy are almost the reverse of ours. In other words, we have in our mission fields about the same proportion who know how to read as we have in North America who do not know how to read. This situation is even more complicated when one realizes that in fields like Guatemala over 85 per cent of the people speak dialects that are not reduced to writing. Of course it must be observed that there are a few people from among the upper class who are well educated.

Such intellectual darkness affords an ideal environment for sin and superstition and abuse. A glimpse into a public market should help us to understand the average intellectual level of the people.

The market places of foreign cities are a sight to an American! Almost any food can be purchased there. It is here one goes daily for his fresh fruits and vegetables and even meats. Also, one can buy staple foods there; however, large quantities are not available. The women, for the most part, have carried large baskets of mixed produce to market in the early morning hours. They do a little dogtrot with the baskets balanced on their heads and their babies in the shawls on their backs. If you go to market after breakfast you will find many people sitting beside their wares, which are spread out on the ground for display.

Among other things, you need to buy some black beans. As a missionary, you now eat beans three times a day and like them. You observe several baskets, trying to guess which beans would be free from weevils. Of course, you have learned how to eat beans with weevils but you would always prefer not to have them. At last you bend over and run your fingers through a basket of nice, shiny black ones and ask the price of them. The lady replies in broken Spanish that they are fifteen cents a pound. You shout an exclamation of horror and start to walk away. She calls you back and tells you to make an offer then, explaining that to talk it over is not costing you anything. At last you can offer her seven cents a pound. It is then her turn to cry out in self pity. She may tell you that you are abusive to offer her less than she could sell them for at a profit. You may tell her that she is untruthful. However, to be called a liar does not seriously offend one of them. She comes down to twelve cents; you offer her nine cents; and at last she sells them to you at eleven cents a pound.

    This marketing is perhaps the principal part of their social life and this bargaining is quite an enjoyment to them; and you, too, will learn to like it if you enter into the process with all your heart. After you come to the agreement, you rather feel that you have bargained her down too far and she may feel that she did quite well with you; so both of you will want to be a bit generous with each other.

    Now she takes out her little homemade pair of balances. They are so typical that I would name them as symbolic of the intellectual status in the mission fields. Being illiterate, the venders could not read the numbers on scales. She measures out a pound of beans, putting in a few and taking out a few and holding the balance so that you may observe too. Then she puts the pound of beans in your container. Now she expects you to pay the eleven cents. Even in the meat market, where the people are clamoring for a portion of meat, an illiterate man will get the attention of the butcher and buy a pound of meat. He hands him all his money, and when his change is counted back he will order another pound and again pay all the money he has. Seeing that there is enough for more, he will order another pound—and so on until he spends up the desired amount of money. This is the way they sell beans also.

An American, thinking to save time by buying enough for a few days, might ask for five pounds of beans. This is a rare thing and the native woman will deal with him in this manner only when she is confident of his integrity. Now she places one bean apart to mark the count of the pound delivered into the container. Then she slowly and carefully balances out each of the other pounds, placing a bean in the line to mark the count for each pound. One must be sure to watch the count himself, because almost all of them would delight in cheating a little.

Having the five pounds at last, the foreigner pays her the fifty five cents; but she cannot accept it, for she has not calculated the price. If she had been paid for each pound one would have avoided this critical moment. Counting and calculating over her five beans with the stranger confusing her, she can never multiply five times eleven, and finally she goes and finds another person in the market to help her. This man will start to work on that problem of simple arithmetic and one can see him "click" as his whole body reacts like a machine as he passes each bean, but he gets the right answer. Then the merchant can take the money in confidence.

Let me mention some superstitions that accompany ignorance. Among their many foolish and ridiculous cures for sickness they will invariably use poultices of some strong leaves. The toad, which gets so very large in Guatemala, is reputed to be very poisonous. If a toad falls into a well, that well is abandoned. Frog soup is supposed to have been used by many a woman to kill her husband. The frog, however, has curative effects on bad infections.

A lady arrived at our house one day with her leg terribly swollen and inflamed. The ordinary running sores that result from the blood condition accompanying intestinal parasites had become infected and she had what we used to call blood poisoning. While Mrs. Hunter treated patients one by one, the others discussed their symptoms and remedies. When I came along, the lady was waxing eloquent in her explanation of all they had done to try to cure that leg. Someone asked if she had used the toad cure and she said they had cured it the night before with the toad. Of course, it was still sore.

I like to see if I can explode their superstitions, so I drew her story out in detail. She explained the process of getting a big poisonous toad and sliding him gently over the inflamed area. If his belly turns the color of the sore that shows them that the toad has absorbed the inflammation. He can then be released and the treatment is completed. I asked her if it worked.

"Oh, yes," she exclaimed, "the toad turned red."

"Certainly," I said, "but the inflammation is getting worse perhaps the toad was simply suffering from the embarrassment of being placed on a woman's leg."

She had a few shots of penicillin and recovered nicely.

Then, there is *maliojo*. Mal means "bad" and ojo is "eye." Now this is not to be confused with *mal de ojo,* which is the pink eye. *Maliojo* (give the j the sound of h) is a bewitchment caused from a strong or evil eye. Babies are supposed to be especially subject to it. Since so many infants die, the people think there is a reason. The interesting thing about it is that the offending party can take away all ill effects if he will love and caress the injured one. This danger is so believed in that everyone who sees our babies thinks he should kiss them. A mother may go after a drunk and have him love her baby a little to eliminate the possibilities of his eye having damaged the child. I was calling one day in strange homes on pastoral visitation and, upon entering, I noticed a crying infant. Its mother was hurriedly summoned and she almost frantically brought the frightened little one for me to love. After I loved it, all was well and they relaxed for a good visit on subjects pertaining to their souls' salvation.

An educated army official whose wife is a schoolteacher came to Mrs. Hunter one day saying that their infant son was stricken by this bewitchment. She told him that he should not believe in such things since he was more enlightened. He said they never had believed in superstitions but were strangers in this interior country and that the local people had diagnosed the baby's symptoms as such. He was frightened for his baby. Mrs. Hunter asked about the symptoms and found that this educated mother had tried to be modern and had put her baby on powdered milk. The milk did not agree with the child. There were not enough hot water bottles to go around, but Mrs. Hunter had the solution to this problem. She instructed the mother to warm the baby with her own body heat for about half an hour. That took away all the *maliojo* for the moment, and then the baby's diet was corrected and it did fine thereafter.

Even little mules and monkeys are subject to *maliojo*. Visiting with some people who were selling a little monkey to my boys, we were told not to take the pretty red ribbon off his neck, for that was there to protect him from any strong eye that should be focused on him. The brightred color should deflect the vision of the offending party. Perhaps we have at last discovered the origin of the use of neckties!

In view of this background, you can see that where the gospel produces its byproducts of intellectual enlightenment and freedom from superstitions such as we in America are blessed with, it is a worthwhile investment of the little bit of money and effort we put into the foreign missions program.

Here is Pedro, who read the Bible through from cover to cover six times in the first three years that he was a Christian. He never had been to school a day in his life. Most of our men will learn to read when they get saved and many of them read the Bible completely through in their first year as Christians. Reading the Bible gets rid of their superstitions. There are our preachers that have been educated in our Bible schools. They are the hope of our future church and their influence will turn the nation.

Not a large proportion of mission money is used for education but the proportion will doubtless increase as the national churches become able to support their own religious program. Long after there is no more need for evangelistic and pastoral missionaries, there will still be a need for missionary educators.

THE HALT

In Latin America the buzzard could be used as the insignia of the Public Health Department. These vultures hold such a place of importance in sanitation (or insanitation) that it is a criminal offense to kill them. I long for the day when all of them will starve to death! Their favorite diet is refuse.

Health and cleanliness have followed in the wake of heartfelt Christianity since the days when Jesus cleansed the lepers and restored the sight of the blind. But in Central America today over half the babies born die before they reach two years of age. If mother and baby survive the ordeal of childbirth attended by a filthy, superstitious old woman, and if they are not seriously affected by the prevalent social diseases, then the baby fares rather well until he takes malaria, is infected by intestinal worms, or maybe until he is weaned from his mother's milk. Communicable diseases are unquarantined and they take their toll too of the already weakened ones.

    One muddy day I was evangelizing in a home where there were two little naked boys. One was nice and fat—perhaps two years old and still nursing. The other was perhaps about four. He was rawboned and thin with a great abdomen. As we conversed, the older boy decided to peel and chew some sugar cane that his father had brought from the field. He borrowed his father's machete (long knife) and ran his bare toe over it to see if it was clean. Now, his toe was naturally muddy because the floor was muddy that day. Wetting the floor is the best way of keeping the fleas down. Just one night in a flea infested house will convince you of this necessity. Waste water is never thrown away. It is sprinkled on the floor. If you stay for dinner you will be brought a pan of water to wash in. You dip up the water in one hand and toss it into your two hands, letting it spill over the dry spots on the floor as you wash your hands together. Anyway, it is best not to get the pan dirty by washing your hands in it, because the soup will soon be served on the table in that same wash pan. Also at the close of the meal you are brought a glass of fresh water to rinse your mouth.

On this occasion the floor was muddier than usual because it was rainy season and as we entered we had apologized for the great gobs of mud that clung to our shoes. However, actually, the mud tracked in makes a contribution to the home, for it helps to build up the floor higher than the street level, so that the rain waters will not flood the house.

Our little friend saw that he left a streak of mud on the machete when he ran his toe over it, so he looked about for a way to clean the blade. He ran it several times over a block of wood that they use for a chair. Still not satisfied, he looked around until he spied a little hen feather stuck in the mud on the floor. This he took and rubbed the machete blade thoroughly on both sides. The machete was perfectly contaminated! Then he stood the cut of cane on the muddy dirt floor and peeled it by wedging it on the knife and hammering it on the slimy floor. When he got it peeled the delicious cane was black with mud. He shared it with his little brother.

The pigs, chickens, dogs, naked children, and often captured wild animals have complete right of way in the house. Such conditions are so ideal for the propagation of the many kinds of intestinal parasites that even we missionaries have to rid ourselves frequently of them. Children almost invariably have protruding abdomens and running sores on their limbs and other general symptoms of anemia as a result of the worms. Often they fall into a delirious fit in which they sometimes die.

Eliminate malaria and intestinal parasites and balance the diet of the Central American and you have an exceptionally sturdy and healthy race. Where our medical missionaries are, we are slowly doing all of that and more.

Next to the actual conversion of sinners, the medical work is the most gratifying of all mission work. It is especially important in the opening of a new mission where the people are really suffering. It is important that the people be permitted to pay something for medical services rendered in order to preserve in them their personal dignity and integrity. Yet it is almost impossible for a man to doubt who has been healed of a bad sickness without exorbitant cost or obligation. Medical missions have proved to be a great entering wedge for the gospel into the hearts of superstitious, prejudiced, sickly people. Where our missionary nurses work, the bodies of the children take on a human shape. A light of intelligence begins to shine in their eyes and the color of their skin becomes normal. The death rate is lowered and the industry and productiveness of the community pick up as a result of better health.

THE BLIND

The cross which Jesus Christ invited His followers to carry, the one in which Saint Paul gloried, was a symbol of suffering. But that suffering results in victory—the most overwhelming victory of the ages. In short, the Christian cross is the insignia of the message of the gospel. It should speak of the only remedy for sin.

But today in Latin America, as in Rome, the cross is on the highest peaks and pinnacles. It is painted on the doors and walls. It marks the graves of sinners and stands at every point of danger or of interest along the byways. Crosses hang about the necks of naked babies and drunken, poverty ridden, ignorant, benighted humanity.

The cross has long since lost its significance as a Christian symbol. However, it does represent a way of life. It represents a fallen, perverted religion. The cross in Latin America today is the token of a religion that set out to control the world, using wicked means to accomplish supposedly righteous ends. The religion of a people affects the standards of living—both economic and moral. Learn what kind of god a man has and you will know what his morals are. By this same criterion you can determine whether or not he is a progressive, industrious, honest, optimistic person. You may largely determine even the health and sanitation of a people by knowing their religion.

Let us look a moment at what is known as the Roman Catholic religion as we find it today in Central America. Though there is at least nominal religious freedom in most parts, the Catholic leaders sternly insist that Catholicism is the "religion of the country." Roman Catholicism has brought into her religion so many pagan customs for the sake of expediency with her modern saintisms and Maryism that she has no right to be called Christian.

    Just a few days before leaving for our furlough we visited the annual festival for the patron saint, Peter, in a large Indian town. Seeing a large crowd gathered about a small idol house, we decided to stop there and give them a gospel service in the dialect spoken there, by use of a wire recording and public-address system. Many people were occupied with preparations for the ensuing days of celebration by making great frames in the streets for decorations. Others were killing a young bull for the feast. The butchers were drunk. They had tied the bull's four feet together and then proceeded to try to find his heart with a blunt butcher knife. Several drunken men were doing the stabbing while others came along and beat the dying animal. Several women were trying to catch all the blood in their half gourds. It was a slow and merciless death and until the last they kept sticking the heart and tramping the animal so as to extract more blood for their blood pudding.

    This butchering was taking place just in front of the house and, seeing people entering, I concluded that it was in public use, so I looked in. There were two large idols in a glass case—presumably Peter and Paul. That case made a good place to preserve the "saints," so they had packed several other smaller images in there too, making the case look ridiculously crowded. Then on either side stood a large crucifix. They were ghastly things! They were made of crossed sticks and clothed with cheap goods. Dust had settled heavily upon them and they were repugnantly dirty as well as tattered, so their pole framework was visible. All this accented the crudely depicted sadness in the faces of their "Christs" and there was horrid red paint splotched on to indicate His wounds. These with a host of other hideous, dirty idols and pictures there at the altar served to bring the drunken people to their knees.

About twenty long beeswax candles burned brightly along the altar railings. They had been placed there by people too poor to buy them when the prayers were begun. The alarming part was that in among the candles worked an altar boy dispensing liquor—pure corn alcohol. There were five men and two women dead drunk and sleeping it off on the dirt floor. Two others were sitting up still but almost ready to fall to the floor for a long drunken sleep.

I watched one woman with a nursing baby in her shawl slung on her back come in and toss a handful of hard-earned small change into the metal plate at the altar. The youth among the candles counted it slowly and tipped the coins into the clay pot on which the plate was placed. Then he gave her a half pint of whisky sealed with the revenue sticker. Others made similar purchases there before the pitiful, unseeing eyes of the idols. When smaller amounts of money were thrown in, the drinks were poured and served out over the burning candles. Two men already drunk came in holding on to each other. They crossed themselves and knelt and prayed fervently in their own dialect while looking their "saints" in the eyes. They occasionally stopped their praying to drink from their whisky bottles and then prayed on. They probably passed out there on their knees, only to be moved back by the altar boy who sold the liquor. Certainly they must have been lying two deep in that idol house before morning. In such times the gutters also are lined with drunk men who fall down and lie dead drunk all night. Sometimes a family will spend more money to pay for a fiesta than the man of the house can earn during the entire year. He then has to sell some of his stock to pay for such religious rites.

    These people have named their babies Peter, John, Mary, Trinity, Conception, Jesus, and Piety. The names of Deity are constantly on their lips, and their business establishments have such names as the Bank of the Holy Spirit and the Meat Market of the Sacred Bleeding Heart. Their religion costs them dearly at such occasions as births and deaths and weddings, but I have yet to see how the so-called "religion of the country" gives anything in return to its followers, except to those who use religion for political advantages.

    Truly they are blind. And this blindness causes the poverty and the ignorance and the sickness. It is a blindness that is the result of idol worship. In their catechism, the vacancy left in the Ten Commandments is filled with a newly fabricated commandment reading, "*Sanctificad a la fiesta*" ("Sanctify the festival").

A new convert will sometimes go to his priest and ask him about this idol worship, reminding him that it is prohibited in the Bible and disqualifies one for an entrance into heaven. The priest will then admit that the idols are not to be worshiped and he explains that they are designed in their "beauty" to help the poor, ignorant soul to conceive of God better. Thus this religion has kept them in ignorance and is doing nothing to enlighten them. The new convert will sometimes remind the priest of this, and some priests have answered that they are trained in their own profession as are doctors and lawyers and it is their livelihood. Since the people get so much consolation from their false notions, they feel no obligation to try to change them, or certainly cannot afford to.

In Psalms 115 we read about idols, and verse 8 says, "They that make them are like unto them; so is every one that trusteth in them." A man can be no bigger than his god. No matter what image it may be, it will stand between the worshiper and the true and living God. It blinds him. St. Paul was called in his vision on the way to Damascus to "turn them from darkness to light." As we do that, we get to the bottom of all their needs.

In our last annual camp meeting last year we saw 128 seekers come to God. In our local churches we are seeing souls saved one by one. Around us some of our neighbors have turned to God. One near neighbor named Genaro Gonzales used to get drunk at every fiesta. He began to listen to the preaching from a hiding place in the shadows outside the church. At last he told me that he believed that he should be able to pray directly to God as we had taught. I encouraged him but made it clear that he would find it necessary to make a public profession and break with the old way of life before God could be known by him as his Father. Little by little the light grew clearer to him. One day he drew me aside as if he were going to ask a most confidential question. He explained that he had purchased one of our scripture text calendars and he wanted to know now if the verse given by each date was the limit for his daily reading. It must have seemed rationed to him. I must have seemed almost sacrilegious as I broke the quiet of the seemingly confidential chat by exclaiming that the Bible is an open Book. I told him to read all he wanted to. The day came when he, along with his wife and their child, sought and found God at a public place of prayer. He is arranging to honor his wife now by a legal marriage, which they had never gone to the trouble to have. They are happy now and are faithful to their church attendance and they are walking in the light. They will have many adjustments to make in this new way of life and they will need a lot of pastoral care. They were typical idol worshiping Catholics and gave me their picture idols after they were saved.

    This is just one of the hundreds of men in our Latin American churches. Out in the interior we have more Christian men than we have

Christian women, and almost every one of them was once a drunkard but is now ready for that "great supper," though they were once poor, maimed, halt, and blind.

Latin America has never enjoyed the effects of a great revival such as those that blessed England and America in days past. The Latin world has not yet reached the place in history of the great Reformation. Those who care for our neighbors to the south and really want something to lift these people should join with those who are earnestly praying and freely giving of their means to take to them the gospel in all of its glorious regenerating and refining power. Foreign missions under the anointing of the Holy Spirit of God is the answer.

CHAPTER X
Four Effective Cures

When Jesus had named His twelve disciples as recorded in the tenth chapter of the Gospel according to Saint Matthew, He sent them out on their first preaching mission with clear instructions to do four other tasks in addition to their primary work of preaching. In verse eight we read, "Heal the sick, cleanse the lepers, raise the dead, and cast out devils; freely ye have received, freely give." Around these four tasks we hereby give an illustrated report of some of the work we have seen accomplished in the name of Jesus Christ under the foreign mission program of the Church of the Nazarene. Since our Lord is always the same, there is sameness in the basic task that He trained His disciples to do and in the task that the Church of Jesus Christ should do today. Certainly if we as a church do not do this work there is no one else who will.

"HEAL THE SICK"

Jesus did much physical healing and had His disciples to do it likewise. In America we have a great medical system to care for our physical sicknesses. This is a product of Christianity. Other countries are not so well blessed. After a few weeks of traveling and preaching in deputation work here in America I seemed to feel something lacking in my ministry. Suddenly I realized that very few people are sick here in America and almost no one has asked me for treatment or medical counsel.

In a previous chapter, I have mentioned the formal medical work that is so important to our missions, but as a preacher I also find it necessary to do something for the sick. Visiting a sick old man named Bias Puga, in my pastorate; I found that both his legs and one arm were cold and immobile. He was bedfast. That is a condition submitted to only by the dying in Guatemala. Finding a man's limbs cold in the tropics seemed to me to be a sign of a fast approaching death. As his pastor, I prayed with the man and later had the church pray for him. From all physical signs, I didn't expect him to live through the following week. Before leaving him I asked what kind of food he was eating and found that he was trying his best to eat a bit of the regular diet of the strong corncakes, beans, and coffee. I told him that he should have some better food at a time like this. The people generally feel that if one cannot live on their good corn and beans he just isn't strong enough to live anyway. But I went to his daughter, who was bringing in his food, and made some diet suggestions. She seemed willing to listen and I felt encouraged.

When I returned the next week end I found the old man greatly improved and up a little. Soon he asked for a Sunday school quarterly and I brought him one the following week. Not finding him home, I left it in his house and on Sunday morning he was in the church before time for Sunday school. When I arrived he exclaimed, "You are the angel that brought me this quarterly. I have all the lessons studied and am ready to recite." The last time I saw him he was away out in the cornfields helping some with the work.

A young man arrived at our door one day sick with malaria and in a severe chill. He asked me to "cure" him. I explained that Mrs. Hunter is the one who treats the sick and that she was away for several days. He insisted that I could cure him. I agreed that perhaps I could but was not practicing medicine nor prepared to do so. I suggested that he seek out the national doctor. He replied that he had been to him the previous afternoon and was told that that was the wrong hour of the day to arrive at the doctor's office. He insisted that he was a stranger and that no one was willing to do a thing for him. He declared that he was dying in his present state. I yielded and promised to look in my wife's medicines for the proper medicines to be given in the case of very much advanced malaria. Upon being told that it would take me some time to prepare, he went out and lay down in the hot tropical sun while shivering with a chill.

By the time I had found the medicine and read up on the dosages and boiled the equipment and called for him, he had passed from his chill into fever and had moved into the shade of the house.

We had taken some long poles which I had cut from the nearby jungle, and with some blankets we had screened off a corner of our house. Some boards on gas cans, two high, served as our examining table in the clinic. After treating him and making him rest a bit, I dismissed him with orders to return for further treatment upon my wife's arrival. He was ever so grateful! Next day I heard a wheelbarrow squeaking in the road and a man whistling an accompanying tune. Looking up, I saw my patient already relieved enough to be able to work a little.

He didn't get saved that day but he came back to finish out his treatments and the fame of the mission spread through him. Furthermore, anyone who is a Christian can talk to that man today about his soul. Perhaps he has already been saved.

Missing one of my best Sunday school teachers one Sunday morning, I inquired about her and was told that Mrs. Lola was sick. After church I went to see her and found her with a towel around her head. There, a towel has ever so many uses besides what we use it for. As there is no need for coats, the people don't use such. However, if a lady is perspiring from working over her cooking or ironing, she will certainly throw the towel over her shoulders before stepping out into the air. If a man should be called out during the night he will need the towel around his throat to keep the dangerous night air from getting into him to cause pleurisy or even pneumonia. A man with a cold never shaves. A woman who has a new baby always wears her head done up in the one family towel for at least the first ten days. When I stay for dinner in a house where there is one such towel, the lady disappears when I wash my hands. A child brings me the towel and I dry my hands and return the towel to the waiting child. Shortly, the mother resumes her duties with the same towel around her head.

So, seeing Mrs. Lola in the towel, I knew that she must be sick. Upon my inquiry she opened her mouth wide to show me the offending tooth. Her lower jaw was swollen badly and she was certainly suffering. We discussed the facts that the nearest dentist is eight dollars away by airplane and going to him is no guarantee of help. I explained further that a tooth should not be pulled while it is so badly ulcerated. She declared that if she could find someone to jerk the string she would fasten it on and have it pulled.

I explained that it might hemorrhage and she disputed by showing me where she had thus pulled one the year before. Sometimes these people suffer with their aching teeth until they gouge their gums away trying to pull their teeth with their bare fingers.

Upon arriving home that night, I told Mrs. Hunter about Mrs. Lola's sufferings. I had to return on Monday to help the men in their construction of a parsonage, so again I mentioned this problem to my good wife. She knows the implications far better than I do and so is reluctant to give me the green light. However, I could not forget that sister's suffering. Before going to work, I got into the medical equipment and got out a pair of dental forceps that Dr. Gerald Wesche had given us before we went to the field. I put them in my pocket and worked with the brethren all day, all the time not being fully decided to venture to pull that tooth. After work I turned the old canoe in the direction of her house instead of going straight home. There was Lola still wearing her towel and, as misery loves company, there was another lady there wearing a towel. She too had the toothache—however, she was not a Christian and I was sure I didn't want to get involved in pulling her tooth while it was ulcerated.

    A good look at Lola's tooth revealed that it was loose and I had it out before she knew it. When I showed her the tooth she began to praise the Lord. It was late and getting dark and I had a distance to travel over the water without a light, so I started to leave. The other lady came begging me to pull her tooth, and at last Lola recalled that she had not paid for the services rendered. She grabbed up some coins and came down the street alter me, asking how much she owed. I told her that I could never understand how a doctor could hurt me and then charge me for it. I can always go to that house and eat. Lola has served God much more ably because of this little act of kindness.

Out in the town of Dolores we were preaching a revival and visiting in the homes of the people with the plan of making an invitation in every home to accept the salvation that Jesus gives. It was the hardest place I have ever worked. One early morning we heard the bells of the Catholic Church and found that there had been a death in the village. We went to the bereaved home and read some scriptures to those poor, illiterate, stricken folks. We told them how our God alone can console the aching heart. We taught them that the innocent ones are safe with Jesus. They seemed grateful and touched by our ministry of the gospel. In that house everything had been cleared out and a table was placed in the center, on which was the little corpse. Candles burned near the feet and a cross stood at the head. It was clear that the little one had suffered from the three almost universal ailments: malnutrition, malaria, and worms. Probably some communicable disease had quickly taken her life in this weakened condition.

    Just as I was ready to depart from the house, I asked how many other children these parents had. With broken hearts they told me that this was the seventh child of theirs to be buried and that only two remained. They get accustomed to the loss of tiny infants, but this girl had reached ten years of age and they had hoped that she would reach maturity. The mother observed that the little baby that remained was sick with malaria fever at the moment and I found that the mother had malaria also. I saw that I should do something more than talk religion to these people. I asked them why they had not sought medicine in times of sickness. For a response they shrugged their shoulders. I told them what medicines to take. I had already found so many sick people on this long trek into the jungles that I was out of medicines except my own dosage, which I am forced to carry at all times because malaria attacks me frequently also. Their plight was such that I shared enough of my own medicine to relieve them of the fever.

When I went to that town I could find no hospitality, as no home was open to us. But when I return again I am sure that home will be open, and perhaps their hearts will be open to receive Jesus.

There are sicknesses, too, that are far worse than physical sicknesses. These are sicknesses resulting directly from sin. Jesus is the only One that can heal them.

"CLEANSE THE LEPERS"

In our evangelization we talked to a man one day who seemed to think it was a joke to visit with preachers. However, as we got into the story of Calvary and made the application to his own guilt and sins and gave him our personal testimony of deliverance, he became very serious and asked, "Do you mean to tell me that your religion can change a man as bad as I am?" We assured him that Jesus can save the vilest sinner. The light began to shine that day that soon led that man to an experience of salvation.

As we came away from there someone met us and asked if we had been wasting our time with that wicked fellow, and explained that we could do nothing with him because he was a bad man. I declared that all sinners are bad in the sight of God and all must repent or perish. This individual explained further that this man boasts of his sins. I said that our Jesus cleansed the incurable lepers and that if this man would truly repent and turn to God he would be saved. I have seen it work in multiplied cases. I can show you a host of fornicators and even several murderers who have been saved and are living righteous lives today.

"RAISE THE DEAD"

I came to know Angelina in one of our newly organized churches. She was a girl of about twenty. I was there to hold an official meeting of the church and, since the illiteracy of the people made it necessary to vote by acclamation and since some who didn't qualify for membership did not understand parliamentary procedure and liked to vote when they had no right to do so, I was determined to know my voters before presiding over the meeting. I was going over the membership list with the secretary when we came to the name of Angelina. As I inquired which one she was, the secretary reminded me as to where she had sat in the last service. I asked about her Christian conduct and he replied that I could judge for myself.

The sore spot in this town was trying to get several common-law couples to get legally married, since they professed to be Christians, and until they married we could not receive them into membership. Since there was no pastor in that church, I thought it my duty to talk to this girl. I asked her about her life and suggested that perhaps she could marry the father of her children. Without more prompting she told me that the father of her biggest boy, a dark, cross-eyed lad, was gone several years hence to a distant city. The father of her little white girl was likewise gone in another direction. The father of the baby lived in this same town but now had another woman and family. Such a mess! Some people can get their lives into such a muddle that no human can counsel them as to what they should do.

We talked to Angelina about the sin of fornication. Perhaps no one had talked to her thus in the light of Christian ethics. For several years since that day she has been serving God as a Christian. She works hard to support those three growing children. The economic stress is heavy, yet she is a faithful tither.

If you could know the helplessness of such girls in Latin America you would agree with me that this is a better miracle than the raising of a body from the grave only to die again. If she remains true to God she will live on forever and ever. If I were a medical doctor I would get discouraged after a few years of very successful practice. No matter how many times the doctor heals a man and prolongs his physical life, that man will inevitably lie down and die. Not so when he is raised from the death of sin!

Except for the miraculous power of the gospel, Angelina would have gone on and on in the vicious cycle of sin that prevails there. Such girls are not let alone. They are regarded almost as public property. Economic burdens accent the need for a mother to have a companion to help her with the family. If someone suggests that in certain instances sin is involved, they will answer that everyone sins. "There is pardon for sin," is the most common expression regarding impurity. And so the process goes on and on. But our God is still doing miracles today and saving even the most hopelessly lost.

"CAST OUT DEMONS"

There are many ways in which the devil manifests himself. God's Word says, "Resist the devil. . ." There is some witchcraft in Central America, and spiritualism is on the increase. The keenest manifestation of demon possession results from drunkenness. The Central American drinks alcohol with the explicit motive of getting dead drunk and entering into a profound sleep. It is not uncommon to find a startling number of drunk men completely unconscious on the streets and in the gutters on the way from one drinking place to the next. This is especially true in times of "religious" festivals.

If I could only capture the screams of some drunk men and let you hear them, you would never be the same again. Some men, instead of going to sleep, go into delirium tremens. They will scream as if they were literally slipping into hell. We have a neighbor who was thus affected. Just a little liquor would take him out of control. Others would get him to drinking, and almost every week end he would beat his wife and babies so badly that they had to seek shelter with neighbors while he was drunk. He had two sets of boy and girl twins. Adam and Eve were the little ones.

    One evening during the muddiest of the rainy season, I had come home after a hard day's work and expected a rare treat of a quiet evening at home with my family. It was so muddy that there was no way to get through the streets to our home without sinking in the mud over our shoe tops. I had cleaned up my feet and changed into some light-colored clothing when I heard a drunken brawl in the street just outside our yard fence. I recognized the voice of this near neighbor, Mercedes. I read awhile after supper and the brawl continued. So before retiring I told my wife that perhaps I should see if I could get Mercedes home. She knew of the danger for his wife, so she went to warn her that Mercedes would be arriving drunk.

    When I appeared at the scene the fight broke up and the opposition retired to their homes, leaving Mercedes with his younger brother trying to protect him by taking him home. Mercedes did not go to sleep nor was he weak when drunk. His brother, though a grown man and sober, could do nothing with him. They would clinch and fall in the mud and wrestle. Seeing that the brother could not handle him, I asked him if he would like some help. He said, "If you please, sir. If you will help me take him home I will tie him up because I can't do a thing with him."

It was obvious that my neighbor was even in greater danger now since he insisted that his life had been threatened and that he must continue the fight. If his opponents had been unarmed up until now, I knew that if he followed them to their homes, they would probably come out with their machetes and injure him, as happens so frequently there.

With a firm grip on his arm and in an authoritative voice, I jarred him about halfway into consciousness and he recognized me. I said, "Let's go home." He walked just a few steps and then rebelled. His brother threw him again and they wallowed in that mud. They were both dirtier than two hogs in a wallow. Their clothing was torn and they were steaming with perspiration. In getting Mercedes to his feet again I got my clean clothes extremely dirty, so I just loaded him up and carried him home. He shouted every step of the way until all that community could be sure that the missionary was out in the drunken brawl. He would scream my name and shout violently.

He was not fit to put into a bed or even into a hammock, so we put him on the dirt floor. I told the brother that I would hold him while he tied him up. He begged and screamed and growled and fought and threatened worse than the old wild horses we used to tame from off the Owyhee range in Eastern Oregon. The brother secured his rope and tied it around Mercedes' arms and legs; but since he didn't know the trick of tying a man, Mercedes loosed himself in a minute. So I had the brother help me hold him while I tied him. That was not a pleasant task—a preacher tying his neighbor with a lariat!

Next morning on the way to work, I stopped to see Mercedes. He was up with a terrible hangover. He was trying to get a packsaddle on his gentle old mule, so that he could get some wood for his wife. He was repentant. But if his wife had been home in the night he would have beaten her with a yard long stick of firewood.

I said, "I'm sorry that I had to do what I did last night."

He replied. "That's all right; in fact, I can't remember much about last night."

"Well," I said, "I had to tie you up, but I did it for your own protection."

We went on as close neighbors for over three years. He could not stop his drinking. His family and friends tried to help him. Leading, upstanding men in the community reasoned with him. They had the priest talk to him and teach him to be more "temperate." Then he got so bad that they had to take him to jail and fine him. All such methods failed. I told him that he needed to get saved, but he was prejudiced against us and our religion.

Once I went to his house with the express purpose of talking with him and his family about their souls. We did not find him home but talked seriously with his wife. However, God had begun to deal with him. It wasn't long until she got seriously sick and had to be sent to the capital city by airplane for surgery. She died there, and we were glad that we had told her the Blessed Story.

Mercedes went to the jungles for the seasonal work of harvesting *chicle* or chewing gum. He is a good chiclero, making good wages at this work. He left the four orphans in care of others. Each week end when he would come in to the airstrip and cash in his gum, the fellows would get him drunk and get all his money, so that he never had a dime to send to those poor little orphans. They were in a deplorable state. Little Adam was so sick that he died before my wife was called to help care for them. All four of those twins would certainly have died had she not gone and given them their medicine with regularity and asked some neighbor ladies to help feed and care for them. They had whooping cough and measles all at the same time plus their malnutrition, malaria, and intestinal parasites.

When the season for working the chewing gum had ended, I was in my study one Sunday afternoon. As Providence had it, it was the only Sunday until then I had been home in that whole assembly year. Mercedes came to my office dressed in work clothes. I thought that he perhaps wanted to talk over some business deal, and I constantly have to remind the people of our Sabbath observance. I felt that I wanted this time for prayer and private devotions, so I was not too warm toward my visitor. Since I had not seen him since the death of his wife and baby, I expressed sympathy. He mentioned his unworthiness to be a husband and father because of his drunkenness. This time he said that he was not drinking at the moment. He told me how he had spent the whole season's cash earnings. He was a bit incoherent and of course did not know our terminology for expressing spiritual ideas.

He told me that he had attended church the night before. I expressed surprise and delight, as I had never known him to go to our Protestant church. I told him that I had not seen him there. He said it was so crowded that he couldn't get in. That was true.

"But," he continued, "I saw some people there in your church who are not what they ought to be as Christians."

"Certainly," I explained. "We invite sinners to our services and want them to get saved; we would like even you to come in."

"No, you don't understand me," he said. "There are some of those who have professed to be Christians who are not genuine."

"Yes," I confessed, "very unfortunately there are backsliders in most every congregation. However, we don't kick them out. We try to get them saved too." I began to try most seriously to lead him into salvation.

It was then that he explained to me that he knew that God was trying to awaken him by taking his wife and later his baby. He told how he had wasted his time and his money in drink, even though he had worked so hard and needed money so badly. He said that his companions in drink had suggested that they all go to another country where they were unknown so they could quit drinking when the money earning season of *chicle* was over. He had been up high in a tall *chicle* tree when the dry winds came and no more of the white sap would flow from the tree bark where he cut it. He knew that the season was over and that he would now have to decide what to do next. He was ashamed to face his little sickly children and the neighbors who knew him. He was seriously contemplating fleeing from the country. What a liar the devil is! Jesus cured a demon possessed man and sent him back to witness to the people who knew him best.

It was up in that old tree that God's Holy Spirit spoke to Mercedes. He did not know how to express it but I could understand from what he told me. He said that almost an audible voice seemed to say to him that he should go right home and get the religion of that missionary and those Protestant people. With a gleam of victory, he told how he had gone down and collected his last little pay check and bought a ticket home on the plane and how he had arrived at church after walking past a whole festival of liquor booths and had not drunk a drop. Something was already beginning in his soul. He had begun to obey God's voice! Like the prodigal son, he kept the resolution that he made when he came to himself.

He humbly asked me if he could be one of us. I instructed him a bit and showed him some scriptures and we knelt and prayed. He was so happy that I'm sure he thought that he was a full-fledged Christian already. However, I told him if he were to combat the wiles of the devil successfully it would be wise for him to make some public profession of his newfound faith. I suggested that he be the first one to the altar that night.

That night the church filled early with people and we set children on the altar railing and on the platform and the aisles were jammed full. They jammed through the big, wide double doors and the windows. I grew anxious about Mercedes. I supposed that the care of those three little orphans had delayed him. At last he appeared in the doorway. He propped his shoulder against the doorsill and stayed put. Often we have attentive listeners in the doorways like that, but the milling and moving shifts them out of focus of the service. Mercedes already had a beginning. God had hold of him. His gaze fastened on the preacher and he heard every word of the message. We made a brief altar call and sang an invitation number.

Mercedes remained there frozen, pale, and stricken. What a picture! I shall never forget it. Out of the multitude that pressed us that night in San Benito, that one man stands out in my memory. He was poorly dressed, as he had no wife to launder his clothing. He had no change of clothing, as all was gone to alcohol. There he stood on the brink of a new life but frozen until he could not move. Seeing that he was not going to be able to come alone, I went back through the crowd to him. He came forward and knelt there while the Christian people lifted their voices heavenward with him. He arose with victory and testified that he had a horrible past but was trusting Jesus Christ for a changed future.

Since then, Mercedes has been attending the services faithfully and growing in the grace of God. Alcoholism and its accompanying demon possession have not once touched him. Those little children who used to flee from his terror like little frightened animals now have an affectionate, tender father. They are beginning to learn to sing the little choruses and hymns of Zion. These would never be learned out in this town in Guatemala except that the Church of the Nazarene teaches them, because there is no other Protestant denomination working in all our field.

We had been holding services once a week in homes near the mission home. We had tried them in the mission home, too, but not many would come. In every case, some would hide in the shadows to listen. After Mercedes was saved, he asked us to hold a service in his house. And when we hung the old gasoline lantern in his house, it seemed that the whole village came. The street was blocked with the crowd outside.

We have the service there each Tuesday night now. What a contrast! A home that was once a refuge for a drunken man who had to be tied on the dirt floors is now a place of prayer.

Men who once thought they had some advice to give Mercedes about how to be temperate are now admitting one to another that the religion that saved Mercedes and is saving other drunk men around us is good for the community, and some of them are frankly considering being saved too.

I am looking for a few people who pray and intercede for souls before the throne of God. Mercedes was saved and delivered from his demon possession only because God spoke to his soul up there in that treetop. Someone prayed for exactly that.

The Church is still able to help save souls. It is as effective today as it was in the day the disciples brought their reports to Jesus. Some things can be done only by fasting and prayer. The real work of the church—the healing, cleansing, raising, and liberating from the power of Satan a sin cursed, lost humanity—will be done only if we as a church do it. There is no other agency in this world that is qualified to do this work. What a shame it would be for us to get on a sidetrack and waste our time doing what other agencies can do.

CHAPTER XI
The Heavenly Vision

Every preacher and every missionary must have a call. One who does not have a call will not stand the stress of many years in the ministry. One who has a call and is obedient will grow stronger under severe trials.

After a year's language study the group of missionaries assigned us to Peten. We chartered a plane for three hundred dollars to carry us and most of our personal effects for an hour northward from Guatemala City. We landed at the Flores air base, which is a central one of the sixteen landing fields from which air freighting is done to and from that department. A few believers were there to meet us. They were disputing among themselves as to where we should live. A church had been divided to form a new one and they never had been fully reconciled. Each church wanted the missionary family located nearby. We lived with one party a few days and then moved nearer the other. We found the work of God disrupted and blighted for lack of missionary supervision.

Years before some native preachers had gone to Peten and preached the gospel. There was a hearty response and many were saved. There was strong persecution, but the work grew. A missionary visited them almost every year but certain difficulties arose that needed attention. When the missionary arrived on his annual tour all would be corrected, but as soon as he was gone the old rut was immediately reentered. I found more backsliders and disgruntled believers who wouldn't even attend church than I found in the church. Organization and procedure according to our Manual were ignored completely in some places. It has taken plenty of prayer and love and tact and patience and skill and in some cases little short of a dictatorial hand to cope with this situation. But, thank God, we have twice as many organized churches today and they are functioning smoothly. Many backsliders have been reclaimed and many others have returned to church and sinners are being saved.

    We had been in Peten only about two weeks when Mrs. Hunter came down sick with malaria and other very serious complications. I had more to do than ever before in my life, but I had to take off a few days and nurse her back to health. Some of God's people were faithful in prayer, or we might not have succeeded even then. Her stomach became so weak that she could not retain a meal. I prepared her something palatable to eat almost every hour for several days. That is no easy task even where anything you could name can be ordered from a store. Out there in the jungles it takes imagination. I learned to cook and keep house for the whole family when I was about eight years old and my mother was bedfast out on the old homestead. Almost all previous training comes in handy on the mission field.

I have had malaria, too. Fever does not bother me, but what the natives call rheumatism gets so painful in my neck and head that I cannot endure the jar from taking a step. That puts me to bed for a day or two. Hauling cordwood to fire a lime kiln, I lifted a log one morning after not having rested properly the previous night and something slipped in my back. Using my numb leg much as a stick, I was able to get into the jeep and home for another whole day in bed and several days of "supervision" around the house. The day before Christmas one year I sprained my ankle very badly at about noon. I walked some on it that day but it kept hurting worse till I was forced to retire early. During the night it hurt so badly that I couldn't bear the weight of the sheet touching my toe. But there was plenty to do on Christmas Sunday. I was pastoring a church and it was having a special feast besides regular services and the program that night. To get there we had a long trip to make by canoe with outboard motor. Before breakfast I made myself a crutch. There was a lot of walking and climbing to do that day. I went up the church steps many times on my hands and the good foot. The ankle was slow to heal but is at last as good as ever.

When we go anywhere except by airplane we have mud to trouble us, and once even a big plane was stuck in the mud for three days. I have worked in mud till I dreamed about mud at night. When working, one is either wet with perspiration or wet with rain. While getting in the lime for the construction of the mission home I got the jeep stuck in the mud so badly that I spent from about eleven in the morning till nightfall working with it. Darkness and lack of gasoline forced us to give up for the night. Next morning I arose early and dismounted the wheels and tires from the trailer I had made out of the spare wheels of the jeep. I made eight bolts out of large spikes and took these items and some cable and chain out to where the jeep was stuck. I bolted these empty wheels onto the outside of the front wheels of the jeep. Then we fastened each end of the cable in the valve stem holes and chained the loop of the cable to a tree far out in front. With the jeep working in four wheel drive, this contraption served to winch it out of its seeming doom. That is the best winch I ever saw on a jeep. I guess we could climb a tree with it if we wanted to.

    I made my lime kiln by digging it in the side of a steep hill. It was rainy weather and the mud was a sticky red. One of the older native preachers came to our house looking for me, and Mrs. Hunter told him where to find me. I was muddy but we carried on church business just the same. But he must have been impressed at finding his white collared missionary in that condition. I testified in the assembly some months later and he jumped to his feet and reported that this young missionary was doing fine. He told how he had gone to look for a man and thought he found a muddy wild hog down in a hole! Well, mud will wash off, you know, and where there is mud there is generally some kind of water.

I have made many treks through the mud in the jungles. The uninitiated are always surprised to find how deep the mud can get and how many obstacles are beneath it. Once during rainy season I had to make a trip out to Sayaxche. I could go part of the way by jeep and the rest was a four hours hard hike through virgin jungle in dry weather. I had sent a message ahead asking some of the brethren to meet me with their pack animals but the message didn't get through in time. I waited in the jungle entrance until it was obvious that not another minute could be spared if I were to arrive at the destination that night. So I took the pack that was intended for the mule and started out. After one begins to perspire freely, the heat does not bother so much; and after one gets accustomed to weaving instead of walking, he goes pretty well.

The reason for this unusual gait is that one can never be certain as to how deep his foot may go in the water filled mule track; and besides, it may catch on a root. One must always be prepared to catch himself with the other foot. Learning of the unsanitary conditions, some have asked me why I don't carry an army canteen and some K rations. I can take them as far as the next soldier, but I am quite content if I get through the jungles in rainy season with just my boots as a load to carry. One old missionary declared that all one needs to "go native" is a blanket and a toothpick. I disagreed with him, preferring to substitute a safety pin for the toothpick. However, most of the time I leave both of them at home if I am to go through jungle mud. I carry only one change of cotton clothes, as it is very necessary to put on dry clothing when one stops exercising.

     Besides the regular missionary work of supervising and directing and expanding the church and the growing office work that a missionary is confronted with, I have often had to supply pastor in some church. There being no building in this area that was anywhere near suitable for a missionary residence, I had the urgent task of building a home. Then in addition to these three major occupations it was necessary for us to produce our own milk and eggs and do much toward supporting ourselves, as the economic situation in Peten makes the cost of living about two or three times as high as in other parts of Central America. Inflation there is leading American inflation. The workmen in mahogany and chewing gum are doubtless the best paid common laborers on any of our mission fields. We hire very little help out there, as it takes the equivalent of the missionary's salary to hire an unskilled man. The cost of materials is even more exaggerated because everything must come in by air. Items of first necessity come for a freight charge of three cents per pound. All other things cost from six to eight cents per pound. Gasoline at six cents per pound, plus the container that requires a return trip fare, costs about sixty cents a gallon more than in other parts. We can buy it wholesale at the airport, if we bring our own container, for $1.05 per gallon. When gasoline is sold by the one fifth gallon bottle, it sells at $2.59 per gallon.

While studying the language near the center of Guatemala, we had been able to save some of our salary. We spent all our reserve in a very few days in Peten. I felt that we had to eat properly if we were going to work and keep well. I adhere to the old theory that food is cheaper than medicine and doctor bills. Mrs. Hunter is a good dietitian and she figured out a strict economy diet. One of our greatest struggles was to have fresh vegetables. Corn, beans, sugar, and some meat are almost always available. Except for meat, even these are much more costly than they are here in America. White flour costs about three times the American price. Except for very costly and very limited tropical fruits, in season, all fresh fruits and vegetables had to be imported to us by plane. There are stores in Guatemala City that sell imported American products at a reasonable margin of profit. From one of these we order some flour and such absolute necessities once a month as we need. High duties on canned and fresh goods make it impossible for a missionary to eat such things that come from America. We have ordered an American apple apiece each Christmas. Some of the time we have been able to get a lady in Guatemala to prepare and ship us a basket of carrots, beets, cabbage, potatoes, and other vegetables, from the open markets in the capital city about once every two or three weeks. When such a basket would arrive we would clear the whole bottom part of the refrigerator and neatly stack the contents in there. The lady had strict orders not to exceed five dollars a shipment, freight and all.

We have tried gardening. With the amount of work we have done, we could have fed the whole village if the gardens had produced as they do in America. During one whole dry season, Mrs. Hunter and the little boys arose early each morning and watered the garden, but it was a failure. We have some tropical fruit trees planted and someday those coming after us will eat of their fruits. We have made our greatest contribution toward better eating, though, as we have taught the natives how to combat insects—especially the leaf cutting ant. Now if only we could teach them to work the year around there could be food in abundance.

The soil is too hot all the year around for plants such as lettuce and peas. Furthermore, if you enrich your soil with fertilizers, that serves to afford greater activity to bacterial enemies of garden plants.

Last year we learned how to produce leaf lettuce. By building one's own soil and hanging the garden, it can get cool enough in the night hours of the rainy season to permit lettuce to grow nicely. If labor were cheap, this would be practical; but as things now stand, it would be better for the missionary to import his food even at exorbitant prices than to produce it in such a laborious manner.

The care of chickens hinders the missionaries from going on trips as they should. Also, chickens are easy prey to both two legged and four legged thieves. Nonetheless, with eggs at six to ten cents each it is nice to hear a hen cackle. Chickens in the tropics suffer from diseases that can kill a whole flock in a few days. Also, the vampire bats are a hazard to them, as they bleed them in the night.

The business of producing milk in the jungles has its difficulties. For an industrial school, this would be an absolute financial success if one could find students who would work. We allowed our cow to run loose in the woods when we first went there. With over a hundred new homes around us, she got into all kinds of trouble. Besides having spent many hours in undignified searches for the cow, we paid almost a total of thirty dollars in fines for her misbehavior. One cow sickened and died, probably from the rabies caused from the bloodsucking vampire bats. Another cow was crippled as if severely burned on all four legs from the sting of spiders. We gave her the biggest shot of penicillin made for human beings and she recovered.

The lumber used to build a house is not to be ordered from a lumberyard, all planed and cut to dimensions. Out there we had to select our trees, fell them, get them up onto a framework, and rip the lumber with two man ripsaws. One man works underneath the log and the other stands on the log. It is hard work. Almost all of the lumber in that mission home was planed by my right arm. That includes doors, windows, and built-ins, besides the door and window frames and countless other items.

Our climate seldom goes below sixty and seldom above ninety five degrees in the shade. That is less temperature change from winter to summer than we may have in the course of any one day here at home. At breakfast time, which is the coolest time of the day, the butter gets soft in the cool season. We recall when our Baby Wanda was learning to eat with a spoon how she would sweat at breakfast time until the water would drip from her nose and run from her elbows to form puddles.

Once I was entering the jungle to bring out lumber with the jeep, over a trail that we had opened on a previous trip. I went alone, as there was not enough work to keep workmen employed. It was to be a trip of about two and a half days of travel in tractor low, with some exercise along the way in cutting logs that had fallen across the trail.

I was going along slowly in the very narrow trail when the jeep bumped a tall, dead tree. It shattered and, before there was time to move, there were tons of dead wood falling on the ground all around. Many a man has been injured and killed in this way. One piece of that tree stuck in the mud and stood planted there quivering. It was the size of a telephone pole. It had not missed my shoulder more than six inches. As I traveled on alone, I started thinking what would have been the consequences if that had killed me. My bones would have been bleached before any other member of my family could have known it. Then I remembered that Mrs. Hunter was also in some danger, since she had gone to the capital city for hospitalization. Our oldest boy, Earl Dean, Jr., was away in the boarding school. Ronnie was at home in the care of a servant girl. Thus, our entire family was so separated each one from the other those days that if some tragedy had befallen any one of us it is doubtful that any other one of us could have arrived before the burial, since the law allows only twenty four hours to bury the dead.

      One of the hardest phases of missionary life has been the separation from our children while they were away at boarding school. When Earl, Jr., was just under six the little school for missionary children began its term. We had a decision to make. If we were to tutor our children at home, that could make impossible the carrying on of the clinical work by Mrs. Hunter. There were advantages in their going away. Their education was sure to be more normal in the midst of other children. The climate of Coban is much healthier. Earl Dean, Jr., completed his first three grades while we lived in Peten. That means that he lived in the tropics less than half the time the rest of us have. He is the only member of our family that has not suffered malaria. However, that means that someone else is sharing his life instead of his parents and that any directing that a parent desires to do is greatly limited. The children have many adjustments to make. I must in all fairness say that God has given us a wonderful missionary in the person of Miss Mayme Lee Alexander. She is spiritual and sensible and takes her work seriously. She does it prayerfully and efficiently. Her work has freed missionary mothers for a lot of unsung missionary effort, and her godly spirit has been a blessing to the children while she taught them.

    The first year Earl Dean, Jr., returned home from school he was accompanied to Guatemala City by other missionaries. They sent a telegram informing us about his travel plan but the telegram reached home after he did. He arrived in our Peten airport and found no one there to meet him, and so he checked in his luggage and walked home. He boasted to the fellows in the office that he could travel alone. Upon finding our house he called to his mother, "Look who's here," and there she looked up in surprise to find her full grown, six year old son returning home from boarding school to surprise us. Then with his "baby" brother, just twenty one months younger than he, he came over to where I was working to surprise me, his dad, and see how the new house was coming. My natural desire was to pick him up and kiss him. But he was too big a man to kiss at that moment.

    Probably the most drastic occasion of testing our mettle occurred when the roof blew off our house. We had just moved into the half constructed house against my better judgment. From the day the cement floors were poured, Mrs. Hunter wanted to move onto them, as they were so much better than the mud floors we had been living on. Our district superintendent paid us a visit and suggested that the economy from discontinuing to rent might well be helpful in construction. Funds for building were exhausted, so I moved in with the expectation of finishing it myself.

  We found no ceiling overhead, no doors, and no windows, as well as unplastered walls. But there was running water installed, as we had built our own rural water system.

  Mrs. Hunter cleaned the new floors and hung some curtains. They were very necessary over the bathroom door and over the bedroom windows, as the natives flocked around our windows to see how the white people live. She even hung pictures on the unplastered walls. I nailed the screen on the outside windows to keep people out, and we made two screen doors and nailed boards over other entrances. We made our furniture out of gas cans and boards. A board on two cans makes a seat. Boards on cans two high make tables and desk. Boards and cans and boards and cans make bookcases and cupboards. In this way we were far more comfortably situated than we had been so far as missionaries, so we decided to concentrate our attention on the work of the church for a while. We were in the rounds of dry season revivals in all of the churches with the help of a native evangelist.

In fact, at this memorable time we were about through with the revival in San Benito, where I was serving as pastor at the time. It was Friday night and Mrs. Hunter stayed home that night to be rested better for the heavy week end of closing a revival. She was not too well at that time.

Just as we opened the service a storm struck. It blew and rained until we couldn't hear in the church. We sang until we could sing no more, and then I put the preacher up to try his voice at preaching midst the noise and confusion of the leaking roof. Just then a man appeared in the doorway beckoning frantically for me to come out. I went out.

The man said, "The roof is off your house."

I said, "It can't be because I put that roof on well. What part of it is off?"

He didn't know. He had been asked to go to tell me in the storm. I asked him about my wife. He knew that she was with some neighbors. With him I made my way through the tangle of wreckage and fallen trees and, sure enough, found a part of the roof way out in the jungle in one direction and another part on the opposite side of the house. I found Mrs. Hunter with some frightened neighbors. They were ungodly people but had knelt and cried out to God in the midst of the storm. After the roof was gone, Mrs. Hunter had beckoned with a flashlight and someone came to take her to that home. She was there to comfort them until the fury of the hurricane passed.

They wanted to get her into dry clothing but had a time figuring out what clothing would be appropriate for a woman that they respected so highly. They had been in British territory a little and knew one English word and also had the article in a trunk. It was a pretty imported gown. I found her dressed in it and resting in a pole bed without mattress, with a dry blanket, and water dripping all around.

I went to the house and worked for several hours during the rain and wind to see if I could save some of the furniture. The beds were all so wet that water dripped through the bottoms of the mattresses. The pictures melted out of their frames and floated on the river flowing out the back door. The chimney was broken off and plugged with rubble. The veneer was curling up on the sewing machine. The organ was getting wet. The books were soaked and their colors were mixing beautifully. Everything was wet! The trunks which were still in use were standing in water about six inches deep. Even the mission money was wet. I couldn't keep a light, so I worked with a flashlight between my teeth. At last I hung up some hammocks and brought the family home to sleep in them.

Next morning we awoke with the sun shining brightly. That is the beauty of tropical storms: the sun really shines when they are over! We dressed in our wet clothing and took a look at the mess. Much mud had washed down off the unplastered, fresh mortar walls. Wet things will mold in a few hours in the tropics.

Mrs. Hunter said, "What will we ever do?"

I instructed her that this would be her day to do absolutely nothing more than to lie down and rest, or at most give some verbal directions to our helpers. She thought this impossible. I asked her who would have done the work if she had been killed the night before. She was very careful that day and suffered no ill effects from the storm.

By dark that night we had the pieces of the roof fitted back into their original positions, so that very few stars could be seen through the roof. We missed the revival service that night, much to my regret. Sunday morning we were all in Sunday school and in all the services of the closing day of the revival. Sunday afternoon there was more wind and I had to wrestle for a while with the still insecure roof; but some neighbors came to help me and we got it weighted down with large rocks until we could get a chance to fix it on Monday. There was good victory in the revival.

Among the Catholic people the talk spread that the fury of God had at last struck the Protestants. When it was at last mentioned to me, I said that it might well be a manifestation of God's fury because it had completely wrecked the new liquor factory. I informed them that I would be glad to patch up the mission home if God needed to tear it up a little while He was destroying the liquor factory. I heard no more about the fury of God. The house is finished now and is well ventilated and comfortable.

This most costly of little mission fields is a ripe harvest field. If we can continue to work there, we should reap a great harvest of souls from the money invested. There is promise that the field will become entirely self supporting in just a few more years.

One day Mrs. Hunter asked me if I had my life to live over again if I would do these things again. I replied, "No, I could never stand it again." But seriously, I am glad that "I was not disobedient unto the heavenly vision." There is more yet to be fulfilled and more to be revealed in this heavenly vision. But of one thing I am still confident: it pays to serve Jesus!

CHAPTER XII
The Harvest

I stood on the review stand and watched my army division marching as one man. As one of their chaplains I could see deep into that military array. I could see ten thousand individuals with distinct problems. I could visualize them as they broke rank and went their several ways, off duty. I could recall case after case as they gained entrance to the chaplain's office after waiting in long lines that they might unburden their individual problems.

I once saw fifty thousand German prisoners in one stockade. I saw a truckload of them mangled in a wreck and I tried to administer first aid to some of the suffering ones. One of them asked us for news of the condition of his home in Germany.

I attended a great mass in Rome and watched many thousands of people filing past the black bronze statue of Saint Peter. By use of panels they were funneled past the statue and each one would kiss and caress the bronze foot. That day in Saint Peter's, the largest church in the world, I saw a capacity crowd. They said that there would be thirty thousand attending that mass. There were no seats. That multitude milled about looking at the statuary. Many had made long pilgrimages and hoped to gain indulgences that would get them out of purgatory sooner.

The Mass was said in Latin, so it was not understood by most of the people. Those who could understand it had heard it a thousand times. Few appeared to listen to the service. That great multitude milled around looking at the sights and commenting on the splendor of it all and filed back out as empty hearted and sinful as it had entered.

Walking home from a Sunday morning church service in San Benito, I saw a young man in the street in front of me. He kept walking slower so that I was forced to overtake him. I greeted him and he fell in pace with me. His language was so broken that we could barely converse because he had only recently come out of a dialect speaking area. But he revealed that he had been listening to the preaching from some hiding place near the church. I invited him to return to church and to come inside. Then just before entering the mission gate I spoke a brief word urging him to get saved. He was in church that night and kept attending. In a week or two he was beautifully saved, and after a probationary period I took him into the membership of the San Benito church. If I had failed to invite him to get saved there on the street I doubt if he would ever have made it. What right have we to exhort a man from the pulpit if we are not willing enough to exhort him in the street?

While trying to evangelize in San Luis, where one language and two dialects are spoken, I was almost defeated one morning by the dialects which I couldn't speak. We had just made an attempt to talk to some people who couldn't understand us and at last they had gone on their way. As we stood there, a young man who understood Spanish came along. My native preacher companion, who is pastor of the nearest church, invited him to attend our services sometime. The young man showed real interest and promised to attend. With that the pastor seemed satisfied and strolled away. But I fell into more conversation with the young fellow. I exhorted him to get saved without delay. He followed the exhortation attentively and after a moment he was a true seeker for salvation. There in the open air beside a big boulder I removed my old white helmet and prayed with that fellow, and I have reason to believe that the supernatural, transforming power of God made a new creature of him that very moment. Why do we complicate matters as soul winners by waiting for some other time or place to ask God to do what He is able to do anywhere and at any time?

      While evangelizing in the village of Dolores (translated "Sufferings") we were confronted with the hardest conditions I have ever worked under. We preached there for five nights and visited in all of the homes, about one hundred in all. People were prejudiced against us to the extent that we had difficulty getting either food or shelter. The services were poorly attended, though many listened from the street. We had hiked in there through deep mud, so we did not have a musical instrument. My helper and I started the song service alone in order to attract the crowd.

But as we went to the homes to evangelize we were well received. I give this one example of the several cases that tell how God gave us success. We approached a little shack where an old man sat reading a book. I greeted him informally and asked what he was reading. He handed the book to me. I opened it in a few places and noticed the chapter headings and made a comment on its contents. Then I showed him my Bible and asked him if he were acquainted with that Book. He was not. I then told him that the Bible is God's message to man. It gives the story of creation. It reveals God's relationships to man from the beginning of the existence of the human race. I told him how man had sinned and that sin is the cause of all our suffering and crime and grief and trouble and guilt. I asked him if he had ever sinned and how it feels afterwards. He conceded that he had and that guilt "bites." Never have I had a person follow a conversation more attentively. I covered the subject in less time than you can read this in English. I told him of God's sure remedy for sin; He, being the innocent One, was crucified in our stead. Ending this very brief message I said, "Why haven't you let Jesus save you from your sins?"

He replied, "I have never heard of that before now."

When I asked if he would like to be saved, he confessed his desire. We prayed with him and then went on with our work of telling the gospel story in home after home where it had never been told before.

Yes, many of them have idols and crucifixes of Jesus and many name their boys Jesus, but they never heard that Jesus paid the terrible price in our stead and is able to save us from a sinners' hell. They never knew that He rose from the dead and rules today and is inviting us and empowering us to be victors over sin.

That very same old man was sitting by my side at church that night. We discovered later that he had gone to an old merchant after our visit and they had dug up an old Bible and verified a lot of things that I had told him. How precious is that Book! But one had been hidden away in that suffering town for many years. It took some hard work to get it into use again.

The entrance into such places as these has been done in spite of adverse financial circumstances. It is away beyond the borders of our lifeline budgets. We can only reach these places and have such precious experiences as we go "beyond the call of duty" and as those who support us pay and then overpay their budgets.

In days past there was persecution where the evangelists went. Once they drilled holes in the bottom of the canoes and let them sink while the preachers were in service. Once they cut the hair off the tails of the saddle mules. Such an act may easily result in the death of a beast where the jungle flies are fierce. Others of our people have been unjustly thrown into jail.

In the early days of the work they found it expedient to worship God with the doors and windows barred. In San Andres a young wife and mother was converted. She was a daughter of the most fanatical man of the town. Through her childhood and youth he had never supported her mother nor even owned her. But now that she had become a Protestant he suddenly took extreme interest in rescuing his daughter from the "heretical, abusive Protestants." He tried to order her to change back to Catholicism. Then the priest tried to argue her out of her newfound joy. At last they persuaded her young unsaved husband to beat her. All their methods failed. Then the old father came to her one day with a threat and warning. He told her that bodily harm would befall her if she went to the next Protestant service. She went, taking her babies. While the Christians were in service a signal shout was given in the street and perhaps two hundred men began to throw stones and roll rocks onto the thatched roof of the house of the Protestant leader, where they were gathered. The Christians knelt in prayer as the rocks began to fall in. The roof was demolished before order could be restored. One of this lady's little boys had his breath knocked out, but none suffered permanent injury.

That little boy and all the rest of the large family including the father have long since been

Christians. Some boys from that family are called to the ministry now. That family gives liberally to support the church. I preached on holiness one Sunday morning in that town and that husband who once tried to beat good religion out of his bride came weeping to the altar and found the fullness of the blessing. Today when we have services in San Andres we open the windows and doors wide. In a recent Christmas service a multitude of attentive listeners gathered on that rocky hill as far as I could see from the lights of the service.

Where the majority of the men there once destroyed the house where the Christians worshiped, today the people have built their own Nazarene church and parsonage. Some of the same individuals who rolled stones then are Christians now.

Last summer we had a baptismal service and I saw the largest gathering there on that lake shore that I have ever seen in any Protestant service in Latin America. There must have been around a thousand people present. Six hundred attended our camp meeting on several occasions, not opposing as they used to, not scoffing as they did more recently. But nowadays a holy hush falls over these great crowds that gather around our services.

Yes, there are multitudes as sheep without a shepherd, even out in the remote parts of the jungles where the population is sparse. Oh, that our hearts may feel compassion for them as our Master felt when He saw the multitudes!

The harvest is passing. It will be lost if we do not reap it. Years ago some missionaries passed through Dolores on mule back and preached there. Many believed. Then air travel to the principal places was made available, so that no preacher passed that way for years. Older missionaries told us of the glorious response they met in Dolores. I could not find one person who would dare to identify himself with us when we entered that town.

We must get the harvest in. In our harvesting we must include the care of the ripened grain. There must be pastoral care for the new converts. We will have to include instruction and direction in the life of entire sanctification until these souls are gathered in to our eternal home at last.

Will you "pray the Lord of the harvest" that we may all together make it possible that we reap abundantly? The losses may show up against our account in that great day of final reckoning.

What is said here is the cry of every missionary from every one of our many fields. Yet God will help us and we can see an abundant and glorious harvest if we will all do our part.

Thank You!

Other Books Available by Earl D. Hunter

Life in a Heathen Village – A description of life in a Nigerian village in 1963-64

Victory Through the White Man's Graveyard – An account of mission work in Southeast Nigeria in 1963-64.

Experiences I Didn't Need – Stories from a lifetime of situations with an element of danger or difficulty.

Please feel free to leave a review of the book online!

Made in the USA
Coppell, TX
18 December 2024